what is economics?

what is economics?

a guide to the world of supply and demand

dan smith

METRO BOOKS
New York

METRO BOOKS
New York

An Imprint of Sterling Publishing Co., Inc.
1166 Avenue of the Americas
New York, NY 10036

ISBN 978-1-4351-5972-3

For information about custom editions, special sales, and
premium and corporate purchases, please contact
Sterling Special Sales at 800-805-5489
or specialsales@sterlingpublishing.com.

Manufactured in China

2 4 6 8 10 9 7 5 3 1

www.sterlingpublishing.com

Design and illustration by Simon Daley

Conceived, designed, and produced by
Quid Publishing
Part of The Quarto Group
Level 4 Sheridan House
114 Western Road
Hove BN3 1DD
England

www.quidpublishing.com

contents

	introduction	6
chapter 1	what is economics?	10
chapter 2	what lies behind economic activity?	30
chapter 3	how does commerce work?	58
chapter 4	how do personal finances work?	86
chapter 5	how do national economies work?	108
chapter 6	how do international economies function?	142
chapter 7	what happens when economics & politics collide?	164
	glossary	186
	bibliography	188
	index	190
	acknowledgments	192

introduction

There is no denying that economics can appear impenetrably mysterious. We all know that economics is important—whether it's concerning how much money we have in our pockets, why our governments behave as they do, or why some 800 million people around the world don't have enough to eat. Yet understanding *how* economics is important is much harder to define.

For an example of the sometimes perplexing nature of the subject, consider the words of the British social commentator and wit David Mitchell, speaking in 2009 amid the collapse of several once-mighty financial institutions:

"The thing is, though, this sort of money, this amount of money, is just some numbers on a computer, sort of disappearing or reappearing... There's no actual stuff. I mean, nothing's caught fire or exploded or sunk or anything... No bad thing has happened. It's not like all the pigs in South America suddenly died of blight. It is just people were juggling with numbers that didn't exist and it got out of hand..."

He was, of course, choosing his words for comic effect but he nonetheless touched on an underlying truth: sometimes economics can serve to bewilder as much as enlighten.

Economics is important because it is the study of how we use all the resources available to us (as individuals and as a society) to meet our needs and desires. It is also complicated because our needs and desires are extraordinarily wide-ranging and because humans are infinitely complex. We may like to think of ourselves as rational beings who work in the best of interests of the world at large, but our decisions may equally be driven by factors including, for instance, greed, laziness, or fear. Economics is, then, a social science—a study of human society and its interactions. The economist, meanwhile, is like a plate-spinner at the circus, attempting to keep in the air the myriad factors and concerns that determine our economic decisions without letting any of them drop to the floor.

This book aims to make the job of the aspiring economist at least a little easier by demystifying the subject as much as possible in a single volume. To this end, the book is divided into seven chapters, each one split into easily digestible sections. Chapter 1 gives an introduction to some of the underlying tenets and characteristics of the discipline. Subsequent chapters deal with everything from how markets and businesses function, to why personal finances matter, and what are the key questions and conundrums our governments face. Together they give a broad overview of macroeconomics (that is to say, how economies as a whole function) and microeconomics (the behavior of individual economic players).

Along the way, we shall look in detail at some of history's pivotal economic theories and their creators—from giants of the past like Adam Smith (the "godfather" of modern economics), Karl Marx, John Maynard Keynes, and Milton Friedman—to leading modern-day economists who are molding our geopolitical landscape right now. There is a glossary of terms to bust the jargon and a bibliography detailing some of the most significant economic treatises ever written. It will, I hope, serve as the perfect jumping-off point from which to delve further into the many corners of the economic labyrinth you are about to enter.

This book does not profess to equip you with all the answers to the world's economic questions. It may even be said that only a fool believes those questions have "solutions" in the normal sense. Spend too long balancing one plate and, inevitably, another will start to lose its equilibrium. That is why economics is so full of disagreement even among its so-called experts. As George Bernard Shaw is supposed to have quipped, "If all the economists were laid end to end, they'd never reach a conclusion." But it is also what makes economics so alive. For all its frustrations, economics informs every aspect of our lives and it matters.

John Maynard Keynes wryly summed it up in *The General Theory of Employment, Interest and Money*:

"The ideas of economists and political philosophers, both when they are right and when they are wrong, are more powerful than is commonly understood. Indeed, the world is ruled by little else. Practical men, who believe themselves to be quite exempt from any intellectual influences, are usually slaves of some defunct economist."

—Dan Smith

what is economics?

money isn't everything

the origins of economics

utility

scarcity

macro- & microeconomics

what's it worth?

the fork in the road

1

money isn't everything

What images does the word "economics" conjure up for you? The first thing most people think of is money—that, after all, makes the world go round. In fact, money, while an important factor, is only one aspect in a much bigger picture.

In broad terms, economics is about how we—as individuals and societies—allocate the limited resources available to us in order to best satisfy our needs and wants. Economists look at how economies (any systems in which goods and services are produced, distributed, and consumed) work. They are also concerned with how wealth (the attributed value of assets possessed by an individual or group) is transferred within society. In short, economics is about how we make decisions about what to produce, what to consume, and how to distribute it.

why is economics important?

Economics is regarded as a social science, since economists investigate how human society and social relationships work. Few of the provable certainties that govern, say, chemistry or physics apply, since human behavior is resistant to such natural laws. But by studying our collective behavior over long periods, economists can pick out trends and draw conclusions as to why we act in certain ways and use that information to predict how we might behave in future.

Such intelligence is vital to us all—not just to governments or big businesses. Each time you go into a shop, you are making a welter of economic calculations. What do I want to buy? What does buying this item prevent me from purchasing? Is the price fair? Is it likely to change? Can I get a better deal elsewhere? So the list goes on…

In order to figure out why we make the decisions we do, the economist needs to master a disparate array of academic disciplines. One moment you will need to be a mathematician and statistician, and the next a historian, political theorist, geographer, philosopher, and psychologist. Cynics have suggested that if you pose a problem to three economists you'll get five different answers. True, economics can be an infuriatingly inexact and apparently self-contradictory subject, but that is also part and parcel of what makes it so fascinating. The chapters that follow try to make it a good deal less mysterious as well.

who invented money?

Although economics is about a lot more than just money, there is no denying that money has a big part to play in the story. It is, after all, something most of us have to deal with every day. But where did it come from? When humans lived as hunter-gatherers, they didn't need money. They simply fended for ourselves. However, when people started to grow crops and keep livestock, they began to trade using the barter system: someone with a goat might agree to swap some of its meat for grain that his neighbor had grown, for example. But, as trade spread and deals got more complex, the cracks in the barter system began to show. Far better to have tokens of fixed value that could be exchanged to secure the goods instead.

So money was born. The first currency (that is to say, a system of money operating in a particular geographical area) was probably the shekel, which was used by the Mesopotamians in the Middle East from around 3000 BCE, with a value fixed to a quantity of barley. It would originally have borne official stamps or seals to indicate the verified weight (and therefore value) of traders' grain. So, rather than needing to find a barter partner to buy their specific commodity at a specific time, people could now trade meat, grain, wine, clothing, jewelry, and even real estate as and when they wished. Soon other currencies took hold, often based on precious metals such as gold and silver. In money, mankind suddenly had, one could argue, the most significant tool for facilitating the expansion of trade, which is why it is often regarded as the engine of economic activity. Money streamlined the process of exchange (i.e. buying and selling) in the market (a term that describes any arena for the exchange of goods and services). When Greece and later Rome dominated Europe between the fifth century BCE and the fourth century CE, money became increasingly standardized and regulated. And it has never looked back.

the origins
of economics

When did economics start? There was, alas, no eureka moment when a single individual came up with the idea of economics. Nonetheless, we can trace its broad historical path and its modern genesis.

The simple answer is that economics has always been with us. From the moment the first humans thought about how they would feed themselves (that is to say, how to make use of a limited resource to satisfy their wants and needs), mankind has been engaged in economic analysis.

However, the modern academic discipline we know today is of rather more recent vintage. The consensus is that it was born in the late 18th century under the combined influence of the Enlightenment and the Industrial Revolution. In the centuries leading up to that time, the philosophy of mercantilism had dominated economic thinking. Mercantilists believed that a nation's prosperity relied on it exporting more than it imported, so that it always had money coming into the economy. In practice, this meant many governments adopted protectionist policies (see page 148), imposing taxes and tariffs to control international trade.

But now the Enlightenment's demand for empirical proof of intellectual precepts combined with an upsurge in production, consumerism, and international trade as a result of the technological innovations of the Industrial Revolution, and a new generation of economists realized the global landscape had changed and that they faced questions and challenges that mercantilism simply could not answer. Indeed, many came to the conclusion that mercantilism was wrong-headed and based on false assumptions, such as the belief that the total volume of world trade was fixed.

the godfather of economics

If one work symbolizes the birth of modern economics it is Adam Smith's *An Inquiry into the Nature and Causes of the Wealth of Nations*, published in 1776. It is difficult to underestimate the impact of his magnum opus, which explored how the free-market economy (that is, a market free from interference from a central authority) contributes to maintaining social order and welfare (see page 17). However, he also argued that governments still had a vital role to play in the economy, notably in providing a portfolio of essential goods and services and also in fostering true competition in the marketplace.

The Wealth of Nations also established such pivotal notions as the "rational" Economic Man (see page 72) as well as analyses of labor and how we go about attributing value to goods. All of these ideas were taken on and developed by Smith's contemporaries and succeeding generations, molding government policy, international relations, and economics as an academic subject.

Not that everybody was impressed. That noted Scottish social commentator, and man of letters, Thomas Carlyle, found the idea that the market should be left to its own devices (and, especially, that slavery did not fit in with this philosophy) anathema. It led him to label economics as the "dismal science," a tag it has long struggled to shift.

Adam Smith

Born in Kircaldy, Scotland, in 1723, Adam Smith studied moral philosophy at the University of Glasgow from the age of 14 and later spent several years furthering his studies at the University of Oxford. Highly influenced by Enlightenment philosophers, he was drawn to the ideals of liberty, reason, and free speech. Having returned to Scotland in 1746, he came to public attention when he gave a series of lectures in Edinburgh two years later. From 1751, Smith was for several years a professor at the University of Glasgow, specializing first in logic and then moral philosophy. During this period he struck up a close friendship with the philosopher, economist, and diplomat David Hume. In 1764, Smith moved to France as the personal tutor of the Duke of Buccleuch, and while there he became acquainted with Voltaire. Around this time he also began work on *An Inquiry into the Nature and Causes of the Wealth of Nations*. In 1776, he relocated to London and published *The Wealth of Nations,* which is now regarded as the first major work of modern political economy and the foundation of classical economics. Among his other most important works are *The Theory of Moral Sentiments* (1759) and *Lectures on Jurisprudence* (1762). In 1778, he became Edinburgh's commissioner of customs, and five years later was a founding member of the Royal Society of Edinburgh. He died in the Scottish capital in 1790.

what is classical economics?

Adam Smith's writings were key in the formulation of what came to be known as classical economics, a school of thought that evolved over the 18th and 19th centuries. Other leading names in the field included David Ricardo, Thomas Malthus, and John Stuart Mill. Although they approached economics from widely differing angles, their ideas fed into each other and nourished the movement as a whole. While highly nuanced, classical economics essentially argues that economic growth and social prosperity best bloom amid a climate of economic freedom. In practical terms, this means that intervention by governments should be restricted. Open competition in the marketplace and laissez-faire trade policies (laissez-faire literally translates as "free to do" and relates to trade without government interference) are the order of the day. While the free market is not perfectly self-regulating, classical economics holds that it is loaded with sufficient mechanisms—principally, the dynamic between consumer demand and producer supply—to balance itself in the end. Of course, there was no shortage of critics of this economic model, not least Karl Marx (see pages 66–7), who believed that the free market was incompatible with social justice and equality because, he contended, it relied on the exploitation of workers. Today, the ideas of Adam Smith and his fellow classical economists continue to be discussed and debated, the questions they raise remaining as relevant now as they were when *The Wealth of Nations* was first published.

the invisible hand

The "invisible hand" was, in short, what Smith believed makes the free market work. As such, it may be regarded as the underpinning tenet of modern economic thought. The invisible hand is an analogy for the unseen force that, Smith argued, ensures economic activity in a free market is coordinated despite the absence of a centralized organizing agent. In other words, free-market economies broadly provide the goods and services that society requires, despite the intense competition for scarce resources.

Smith described the invisible hand in *The Wealth of Nations*. Writing in a world still dominated by mercantilist theory, which called for government intervention to maintain economic harmony, Smith's assertion that economies work best when driven by the counter-balancing self-interest of individuals was revolutionary. He said that in a free market competition ensures suppliers will provide the goods and services wanted and needed by the most people, even when suppliers have no personal connection or goodwill toward the consumer. Instead, it is the supplier's own self-interest and desire for wealth that impels them to provide what the market demands. Similarly, it is the self-interest of consumers that drives them to purchase from suppliers that they don't necessarily know and toward whom they don't have any goodwill.

the greatest good

Thus, under the guidance of the invisible hand, the self-interest of individuals drives the market to meet the needs of society as a whole, providing the greatest good for the greatest number of people. In Smith's own words:

Every individual necessarily labors to render the annual revenue of the society as great as he can. Generally, indeed, neither intends to promote the public interest, nor knows how much he is promoting it… by directing that industry in such a manner as its produce may be of the greatest value, he intends only his own gain, and he is in this, as in many other cases, led by an invisible hand to promote an end which was no part of his intention. Nor is it always the worse for the society that it was no part of it. By pursuing his own interest he frequently promotes that of the society more effectually than when he really intends to promote it. I have never known much good done by those who affected to trade for the public good.

While Smith held that markets generally work best when they are free from government interference (which would inevitably obstruct the invisible hand), he still backed state intervention in certain areas—including health and education—where he doubted the ability of private enterprise to provide for society at large.

utility

As we have seen, economics is about balancing our limitless wants against limited resources. In this section, we will consider the first half of that equation by looking at a key concept: utility.

Utility, in economic terms, refers to the total amount of satisfaction or happiness that is gained from consuming a good or service. There is an assumption that human beings generally make decisions that bring them the most happiness in a given set of circumstances.

That might sound like common sense, but the reality is, needless to say, much more complicated than that. For a start, how do you measure utility? The classical economists were hopeful that in the future psychologists would be able to define a method, but this is still an unfulfilled dream. One day our understanding of how the brain processes satisfaction may be so advanced that we can attribute a specific value to an individual's level of happiness. But, even while we wait for that breakthrough, the concept of utility serves a valuable purpose.

Utility allows economists to give sensible, if imperfect, consideration to a subject as complex as happiness. It allows a general comparison of levels of satisfaction. Without the concept of utility, where would we begin? What is happiness? Why are our experiences of it so different? Does eating a chocolate bar make you happy? As happy as falling in love? And why does a roller-coaster ride make one person feel exhilarated and another person miserable? Consider, alternatively, the person who feels a warm fuzzy glow when they give money to a charity and compare it with the resistance of someone else to part with any of their hard-earned cash.

are you really happy?

Economics envisages that the consumer decides what to consume (and at what cost to themselves) in order to maximize their utility. According to the market-economy model, the market will provide those things that bring most people the most happiness, ensuring that the world's limited resources are used to their best advantage.

However, critics of the free market rightly point out that this system has obvious faults. Take the example of a chocoholic—let's call her Coco. Coco may feel that chocolate brings her so much happiness that she is happy to pay for and consume ten large bars per day. However, over the long term Coco's addiction makes her overweight and susceptible to ill-health. In those terms, chocolate may be seen to have detracted from her happiness, not added to it.

Furthermore, the money she has spent on chocolate in the apparent pursuit of happiness cannot then be spent on something else that might have brought her greater long-term benefit (e.g. a gym membership). Meanwhile, all those ingredients that went into the chocolate Coco consumed could not be directed toward providing a genuinely hungry person with essential sustenance. Coco's pursuit of happiness has not worked in her interest, nor has it led to a sensible use of limited resources.

This is why economists talk about marginal utility—how our levels of happiness are affected by incremental increases in our consumption of a particular good or service. Coco's utility might be increased by eating one bar per day, and perhaps even two, but before long her increased consumption gives diminishing marginal utility. The more she consumes, the less benefit she gets with each new bar.

anyone for a marshmallow?

In 1970, a team of academics at Stanford University in the U.S. conducted a series of hugely influential experiments into how we make decisions concerning our consumption. A group of children aged three to six years old were offered a treat (most famously a marshmallow) but with a set of conditions attached. They could either eat the treat straightaway or else resist temptation for 15 minutes, at which point they would be given an additional treat. Of some 600 test-subjects, about a third managed to pick up the extra reward. The study was of great interest to economists for its insights into delayed gratification. Why do some people have the self-control to forgo immediate pleasure for a greater level of utility later, while others would rather have an instant but lesser hit of joy? Evidently, psychology and personality are pivotal to our understanding of utility and why we make particular economic decisions. Coco, take note!

scarcity

If we had endless resources, economists would be out of a job. We could have as much as we want, and there would still be more to go around. But, because resources are limited, "scarcity" is the next key word in our economics lexicon.

In economics, scarcity refers to a shortage of something that is in demand. And pretty much anything we need to pay for is subject to scarcity. From copper and oil to bread and water, demand outstrips supply, globally if not locally. The greater the competition for a resource, the higher its price.

Limited natural resources are an obvious cause of scarcity. For instance, the amount of food grown in the world may be limited by the amount of land and labor available. The problem is compounded by developed countries (with more money to spend) taking a larger proportion of the food available, while less developed ones face food crises (i.e. scarcity). Within those developing countries, the price of food then rises, leaving the poorest to go hungry. As we see all too regularly, a natural disaster or political or social turmoil can make poorer countries vulnerable to mass starvation.

why we go short

Scarcity also results from technological shortfalls. There are those who believe that eventually GM (genetically modified) crops will ensure a global food surplus as crops become hardier and nutritionally improved. More people, the theory goes, will be fed by crops grown using less land and labor. But for now, the technology is still in its development phase, and there are myriad legal and ethical concerns about GM food to consider. Furthermore, those countries suffering the worst food crises often lack the finances to introduce technology to improve their lot. In much of the developing world, people still rely on subsistence agricultural practices that disappeared from developed nations a century or more ago.

A third contributory factor to scarcity is lack of time. A farmer tending his plot cannot be elsewhere sourcing water or prospecting for oil. Of course, scarcity affects rich and poor alike—but differently. The farmer in sub-Saharan Africa chooses between buying a goat or grain, or perhaps even a mobile phone; the merchant banker in New York ponders whether to splurge on a Porsche or a Ferrari. Very different decisions—but economic quandaries resulting from scarcity nonetheless.

water, water everywhere...

There is a growing school of thought that the scarcity of that most basic requirement for life—water—poses the greatest threat to global security in the 21st century. As of 2014, it was estimated by the charity WaterAid that 650 million people lack access to safe drinking water. The threat is particularly acute in the Middle East, North Africa, and southern Asia, exacerbated by increasing demands on what water there is. Not only do we drink it but we use it in ever vaster quantities to water crops and for industrial processes. Some governments have sought to increase and protect their water resources by building vast dams, but these often restrict the water supply to neighboring countries, leading to international tensions. Egypt and Ethiopia, for instance, have been at loggerheads over just this issue in recent years. The struggle for control of water resources could also lead to internal conflict within a country, particularly where ethnic and tribal tensions exist. As Peter Gleick, President of the Pacific Institute, noted in 2014: "I think the risk of conflicts over water is growing—not shrinking—because of increased competition, because of bad management, and, ultimately, because of the impacts of climate change." The battle for water thus illustrates how resource scarcity is a crucial real-world issue.

21

macro- & micro-economics

There is no single right way to study economics, but it is useful to think of it as consisting of two major components: macro- and microeconomics.

Macroeconomics is the "big picture" part of the subject. It takes an economy as a whole—whether local, regional, national, or international—and looks at how all the constituent parts work together and influence each other. Think of all the stuff you see on the news about government and the economy—from inflation and interest rates to unemployment and the balance of trade. Macroeconomics is also concerned with how and why economies grow and contract and what governments can do to spur the former and minimize the latter.

The chief weapons of government in that ongoing battle are fiscal policy (that is to say, how the government collects taxes and spends money) and monetary policy (how governments, via central banks, influence the supply of money within the economy).

Microeconomics, meanwhile, is all about the detail. How do individual consumers behave, and why do they make certain decisions? What influences their spending, saving, and investing patterns? Equally, how do businesses go about succeeding in the marketplace? Unlike its macro counterpart, microeconomics does not make the headlines, but it is there in your bank statement, in your pension prospectus, and in your employer's annual report.

twin disciplines

While some economists will become particular experts in one or other of these two fields, the two disciplines should never be thought of as entirely separate. In fact, they are intimately related—the actions of government, individuals, and businesses influence and feed into one another all the time, so that any given economy is in a constant state of flux. Furthermore, macro- and microeconomics both wrestle with the same basic questions of how resources are allocated. They are more like non-identical twins than distant cousins!

In key respects, microeconomics today deals with many of the same concerns as it did a century ago. While what we consume changes, our behavioral patterns are subject to much the same influences. Whatever historical period you look at, consumers have always sought out the best deal for themselves. They want to pay as little as possible for the maximum utility. Businesses, conversely, are almost always driven by a desire to maximize profits. The microeconomic dance takes place to this unchanging tune.

Macroeconomics, by contrast, gets evermore complicated as our world becomes more interconnected. In times past, governments needed to pay relatively little heed to what was going on in foreign economies unless that economy was a particularly important trading partner. Today, though, an economic change in one economy can have enormous repercussions for what happens in the wider world. Consider, for instance, how the travails of the Greek economy have threatened to derail the entire European Union project since 2010. Or how a change of circumstances in the Middle East can impact the oil trade and thus the economic prospects of countries thousands of miles away. We will look at microeconomics in more detail in chapters three and four, with the focus turning to macroeconomics in chapters five, six, and seven.

why does the global slowdown matter so much to economists?

When the global economy went into meltdown in 2008, it undermined an array of economic "truths" that had been held dear for many years. It also showed how macro- and microeconomics interrelate. The catastrophe was set in motion by the decline of the U.S. housing market, the result of a misguided willingness by individuals to take on levels of personal debt that they could not afford and for banks to offer them credit. These were microeconomic failures. Before long, though, the problems had "gone macro" as governments were compelled to bail out financial institutions for fear that their entire economies might collapse. Then the debate raged as to how to get things back on track. Should it be left to the markets to right themselves? Should governments try to spend their way out of impending recession (an example of fiscal policy)? Or should they flood the economy with new money in the hope of restoring equilibrium (an example of monetary policy)? It is a conundrum that economists are still puzzling over in the hope of averting another such crisis. Whatever the answer, it involves a deep analysis of both the micro and macro aspects.

what's it worth?

Why do things cost what they do? How come, for instance, we pay the same for a cup of coffee on main street as we might pay for a book or an umbrella?

We have already looked at utility as a measure of the satisfaction that a good or service gives us. But, of course, we do not pay for things in units of utility. Instead, we attribute a price—its market value, usually described in terms of a currency such as the dollar, pound, or euro.

So how are values assigned to specific goods and services? In theory, market value is the price at which a good or service would sell at a competitive auction— its value is, ultimately, what someone is prepared to pay.

However, if we are to follow this argument through to its logical conclusion,

we should surely attribute the highest prices to those things most vital to us. Water and food staples should by rights be of more value to us (since without them we would die) than diamond rings or designer shoes. Yet we generally pay much more for luxury goods than life's essentials.

There are other factors at work, then. First, as we have already seen, there is the matter of scarcity. In the developed world, there are enough of the staples of life that prices remain low. Furthermore, there is often a social contract that ensures that a resource such as water is made available at relatively low cost to the consumer.

value in exclusivity

By contrast, jewels from de Beers or Louboutin shoes are in much scarcer supply, so competition to own them is thus much fiercer. Of course, if we found ourselves in the desert and without water, we would much more likely give our worldly goods for a bottle of water than a pair of upscale shoes. And yet, in reality, most of us have a reasonable expectation of accessing water whereas only a few of us will ever sport a pair of Louboutins. So the shoes are attributed a higher value price, even though they may be of less intrinsic value than, say, water.

Other factors come into play, too. How much work went into producing a good (epitomized by the labor theory of value espoused by the likes of David Ricardo and Karl Marx)? How long will an item last? A tailored suit that will go on for years will generally command a higher price tag than an off-the-rack number that starts to split after a few months. Buyers also consider how well a product retains its value. An average pair of factory-made shoes rapidly reduces in value once you have worn them a few times; those Louboutins, however, will command a much higher sell-on price if you decide to offload them. Our attribution of value also reflects fashion and fads—a dress or piece of furniture sold at a premium price one year may be valued at much less the next year simply because tastes have changed.

The value the market gives a good or service, then, is a complex reflection of a range of considerations—how happy it makes the consumer, how rare it is, how well-crafted, how novel, how long-lasting, how widely admired, to mention but a few.

what's in a name?

While market value is not solely subject to the whims of consumers, the influence of personal taste and socially constructed standards of value should not be underestimated. Why is gold, for instance, regarded as intrinsically far more valuable than, say, tin, which has all sorts of superior practical applications? Gold's value ultimately results from a social consensus built up over millennia that it is the default "store of value." In the same way, we agree that a five-dollar bill is worth more than a one-dollar bill, not because the bill itself is of intrinsic superior value but simply because we, as a society, find it useful to agree that it is worth more. If that seems rather arbitrary, it is! But there is often a disconnect between an object's assigned value and the utility we get. For example, currently the world's most expensive standard bottle of wine is a 1787 Château Lafite (a bottle sold at auction for $160,000 as long ago as 1985). Yet experts agree that anyone who drank the wine now might as well knock back a bottle of vinegar instead. The bottle of wine as a tradable commodity has thus been assigned a value far beyond that which it would command merely on the basis of its qualities as a drink to imbibe.

you can't have it all

The term "opportunity cost" was coined by an Austrian economist, Friedrich von Wieser, in his 1914 work, *Foundations of Social Economy*. He believed that the real value of something was in what was sacrificed to get it. It is a rather glass-half-empty way to view the world but has gained wide acceptance over the years. However, over 150 years earlier, Benjamin Franklin had reached much the same conclusion when he famously stated that "time is money" in his *Advice to a Young Tradesman*: "He that can earn Ten Shillings a Day by his Labour, and goes abroad, or sits idle one half of that Day, tho' he spends but Sixpence during his Diversion or Idleness, ought not to reckon That the only Expence; he has really spent or rather thrown away Five Shillings besides." Or, as Lionel Robbins put it amid the global economic upheaval of the 1930s: "Economics brings into view that conflict of choice which is one of the permanent characteristics of human existence." Advertisers, politicians, and eternal optimists might insist that we can somehow have it all, but economists know not to trust the peddlers of such dreams. If von Wieser is right, even if we could have it all then we would have no way of recognizing the value of anything anyway.

"opportunity cost"

Opportunity cost is what we lose when we choose one option and forgo the next best. It is, in other words, the benefit we sacrifice in order to take up our preferred opportunity. All of us listen to the nagging voice telling us what we might have had every time we make an economic decision.

For instance, if you go to a shop and buy a loaf of bread, you cannot use the money you just spent on a bottle of drink. The drink is the benefit forgone—the opportunity cost. In the same way, the opportunity cost of that weekend away in Paris is the utility you would have got if you'd gone to your second choice destination, Amsterdam, instead.

While we may take such a low-level opportunity cost on the chin, the stakes are often considerably higher. If a child needed an expensive medical operation, should their parents sell the family home to pay for the treatment? Is it an acceptable pay-off that the other children in the family enjoy a lower standard of living to give their sibling a chance of better health? Such decision-making can be excruciating.

what matters most to us?

Governments, too, are constantly evaluating opportunity costs as they seek to spend their limited budgets, sometimes with life-and-death consequences. Granting the money to build a new school or open a theater might result, for example, in the opportunity cost of an unbuilt hospital or the closure of existing wards. Similarly, is it more important to invest in your military capability than to use the same money to rejuvenate transport infrastructure or train more teachers? Every government struggles to balance the many competing needs of society, and a good one must constantly weigh up the relative opportunity costs of every decision it makes.

Nor is opportunity cost a phenomenon faced only by consumers. Businesses must also factor in the opportunity costs of production. Consider, for example, Farmer Brown, who has a large field at her disposal. She must decide whether to use it to grow wheat or potatoes. She must calculate how much profit she thinks she will make by pursuing each option, taking into consideration the costs of cultivation. If potatoes offer greater returns, Farmer Brown will sow her field accordingly, but the profits forgone by not growing barley constitute the opportunity cost she must keep in mind.

Meanwhile, the shopkeeper who uses a shelf to stock Farmer Brown's potatoes must consider the opportunity cost of other competing products that he now does not have room to stock. How much profit might he have made by supplying Farmer Giles's carrots instead? And when Old Mother Hubbard visits the shop to restock her cupboard, she ponders the onions she will not be buying with the money she spends on the potatoes. Opportunity cost is thus the specter that stalks producers, suppliers, and consumers eternally.

the fork in the road

When it comes to looking at the really big questions of economics, economists are often said to come from either an "orthodox" or "heterodox" school of thought. But what do these, admittedly rather vague, terms mean?

The first thing to understand is that these two terms cover a multitude of theoretical and intellectual approaches. You could fill one room with supposedly orthodox economists and another with apparently heterodox ones, and you will have as much disagreement in each room as if you had populated them randomly.

Nonetheless, there are some clear commonalities between members of each group. Orthodox economics—sometimes called mainstream economics—broadly encompasses the principles of the neoclassical economic tradition. According to the neoclassical model (which, in the 20th century, grew out of and succeeded the classical economics of Adam Smith et al.), all economic agents are rational—individuals want to maximize their utility, firms want to maximize their profits, and agents have access to all the information necessary to make informed decisions.

The 1940s saw the appearance of a variant of the neoclassical model, neoclassical synthesis, which merges a neoclassical approach in microeconomics with a Keynesian approach in macroeconomics. Orthodox economics is, it might be said, the sort of economics that is routinely taught on postgraduate courses, rooted in a general consensus as to how economies work.

On the other hand, heterodox economics takes in all those approaches that fall outside of orthodox schools of thought. Inevitably, then, both the orthodox and heterodox branches of economics are very broad churches. Heterodox economists often embrace wider social and historical factors in their economic analysis and are skeptical of the veracity of standard neoclassical assumptions. Heterodox economics, for instance, routinely doubts the rationality of economic players and questions the notion of inherent equilibrium within economies. Meanwhile, governments are regarded not as merely additional economic agents but as political and historical institutions that bring a multitude of political and social assumptions and values into the economic sphere. In recent decades, heterodox economics has been characterized by an increasing pluralism that attempts to reconcile seemingly distantly related or even opposed economic positions.

off the beaten track

Among the most notable economists to be labeled heterodox is Karl Marx, on the basis of his rejection of the classical economic model that Smith outlined. With vastly different views to Marx, but nonetheless widely regarded as heterodox, was the Austrian School that emerged in Vienna at the end of the 19th century. It was founded by Carl Menger, whose 1871 *Principles of Economics* approached the subject from revolutionary new angles—for instance, ruminating on the subjective value of goods and services. Other, more recent, examples of heterodox approaches include feminist economics (focusing on the interaction between women and economic structures, particularly in light of traditional male bias) and environmental economics.

the noble prize?

Arguably the greatest accolade available to economists is the Nobel Prize for Economics. Unlike other Nobel prizes, it was not established by Alfred Nobel himself but has been awarded since 1969 by the Royal Swedish Academy of Sciences using a grant from the Sveriges Riksbank, which celebrated its 300th anniversary in that year. In line with the principles that have governed all Nobel prizes since 1901, it goes to the individual or individuals deemed to "have conferred the greatest benefit on mankind."

However, the prize has plenty of critics. One winner, Friedrich Hayek (see pages 114–15), went so far as to use his prize-winner's speech in 1974 to state that he would have advised against its very creation, claiming it "confers on an individual an authority which in economics no man ought to possess." Most commonly, the Academy is accused of upholding the dominance of orthodox economic schools of thought. In some respects, the statistics do not speak well for the organizers. For instance, of the 75 laureates to have been awarded the prize up to 2014, only one had been a woman (Elinor Ostrom in 2009). With laureates' average age being 67, and over two-thirds claiming U.S. nationality, there is the inescapable feeling that winners tend to fit a certain profile. Nonetheless, the Academy has conferred the prize to both orthodox and heterodox economists. Not least among the latter was Hayek himself.

what lies behind economic activity?

the markets

prices in a perfectly competitive market

capital

the Kuznets curve

types of economy

sustainable growth

creative destruction

economic bubbles

wealth

accounting

forecasting

the markets

In simple terms, a market is a space in which buyers and sellers come together to trade goods, services, or other assets. Markets keep the worldwide economy moving, but there's much more to it than selling fruit and veg.

As soon as humans began rearing animals and growing crops, they began to trade, and the idea of the market was born. Where once virtually every town or village of any size had a market square, modern equivalents include town-center shops, the supermarket, the out-of-town retail park, and, increasingly, cyberspace. Other "physical" markets include wholesale markets, where merchandise is traded in bulk to retailers who then sell it in smaller volume to end-buyers. Then there are highly specialized markets, such as those dealing in real estate and jobs. A market in which trading is done without government intervention as to price or quantity traded is known as a free market. Markets that subvert government regulation, meanwhile, are known as black markets.

While physical markets are easy enough to conceptualize, financial markets are much more opaque, yet financial trades amount to trillions of dollars every day. Many of these markets now operate around the clock, with assets bought, sold, and resold within a matter of seconds. This tends to be done in one of two major ways: over the counter between two parties, often using a broker; or on an exchange, which provides a trading platform and where commodities are listed and trades recorded. Some financial trades deal in futures, which commit both sides to a deal at a set price at a future date, with investors hoping that their fixed price will better the actual price on that date. An option, meanwhile, gives the holder the choice of selling at a future date at a prearranged price if it is advantageous to do so.

major types of financial market
- **The money market—dominated by financial institutions and a few giant**

firms, this allows for short-term loans of generally large sums of money. Because the sums involved are so big, the lender will profit even though the rate of interest may be low.

- The bond market—where bonds, predominantly issued by governments and companies, are traded. A bond guarantees an investor repayment (plus interest) at a set future date. Bonds vary in risk from the very safe (government "gilt-edged" bonds and "investment-grade" bonds issued by private companies) to those in danger of default ("junk" bonds).

- The equities market—in which stocks and shares (holdings in companies) are exchanged between institutions and individuals. Shareholders are entitled to a cut of a company's profits in accordance with the size of their holding.

- The foreign-exchange market—traders hope to take advantage of fluctuations in the exchange rates between different currencies in order to turn a profit. For instance, a trader might buy a quantity of pounds sterling and sell U.S. dollars in the hope that the pound will appreciate against the dollar.

- The commodities market—commodities are generally agricultural and mining products sold in bulk, and these may be "soft" (food crops, for example) or "hard" (oil and gold). Profits result from predicting fluctuations in the global commodity price.

what is the LIBOR scandal?

For evidence of how important the financial markets are, look no further than the LIBOR scandal that came to light in 2012. LIBOR stands for the London Interbank Offered Rate and is a figure issued at 11 a.m. each day in London that sets the benchmark for how much it will cost banks to borrow money from one another. The calculation was based on estimated figures provided by the banks as to how much interest they are paying or expect to pay each other. It is thought that deals worth $450 trillion are determined by the LIBOR.

If you think that all means nothing to you, think again. Banks need to borrow from one another all the time to ensure they hold sufficient liquid assets at any given moment, and a change in the LIBOR has knock-on effects on, for example, corporate loans, mortgage rates, and credit-card costs.

In the 2010s, allegations surfaced that many leading banks had set about manipulating the rate for their benefit and to the detriment of their customers and the global economy. As of 2015, such illustrious banking names as Barclays Bank, JP Morgan, Royal Bank of Scotland, UBS and Deutsche Bank had been fined by regulators for what was, in effect, market manipulation. The rate is now set on the basis of recorded transactions rather than bank-submitted estimates.

prices in a perfectly competitive market

Alfred Marshall's *Principles of Economics* was a founding document of neoclassical economics and remains a basic text for students of economics. Among his many important theoretical contributions was the idea that markets, not businesses, dictate price.

Marshall was a pivotal figure in explaining how the basic forces of supply and demand correlate in the marketplace and tend toward a general state of equilibrium (see Give & Take, page 60). He also evolved important new concepts such as marginalism (the study of how much additional use/utility is derived from an incremental increase in the supply and/

or consumption of a good or service), consumer surplus (when the utility a consumer gains from a product leaves them willing to pay more for it than the market price) and the representative firm (a single firm representative of an entire industry). In addition, Marshall brought scientific and mathematical rigor to his analysis, yet he wrote with a clarity that appealed to economists and non-economists alike.

One of his greatest insights was that market forces determine price. That means that firms in a competitive marketplace are unable to be price-setters (they cannot set a price that allows them to make profits above a "natural level") but are price-takers, accepting the market price as a given.

all things equal

To explain his thesis, Marshall developed an economic model which we call "perfect competition." This describes a theoretical and idealized market in which all businesses are selling identical items and are free to leave or join the market at will; each economic agent on both the supply and the demand sides has access to all relevant information (including market price); and there are so many consumers and suppliers that the individual transactions of any of them are insufficient to affect the market price. In reality, no such market scenario exists, although it remains a useful construct for analyzing specific scenarios.

In our perfect market, if any one business attempts to raise their prices, consumers will go to cheaper competitors, and the business will sell nothing. Meanwhile, if a business lowers its price, it will not enjoy extra demand since it remains but a tiny component of a vast market. Instead, each business must calculate the optimum level of output to maximize its profits (the volume of output immediately before the point where the cost of producing additional units surpasses the selling price). A united attempt by all suppliers to raise profits by increasing prices could only ever succeed for a short while before new companies entered the market, increasing supply and forcing the price down again. In a perfect market, then, price is determined by the combined actions of all consumers and producers, forcing businesses to accept the market price.

Critics of Marshall's perfect-competition model claim it has nothing to do with the sort of profit-motive-driven competition envisaged by the classical economists, where businesses attempt to outdo each other, perhaps by reducing production costs or offering a superior product. Instead, Marshall imagined a world of passive entrepreneurs selling the same products, produced at the same cost, and retailing at the same price. Nonetheless, his model remains a staple—albeit imperfect—of modern economic understanding.

Alfred Marshall

Alfred Marshall was born in London in 1842 and won a scholarship to St. John's College, Cambridge, where he excelled in mathematics and also studied metaphysics and ethics. A utilitarian, he was drawn to economics, which he saw as a way to bring about improved conditions for the working classes. He became a fellow of St. John's in 1865, and three years later was appointed lecturer in moral sciences.

In 1877, he married Mary Paley, and took up the post of principal at University College, Bristol. In 1879, he and Paley jointly published The Economics of Industry. In 1885, he returned to Cambridge as professor of political economy, a position he maintained until his retirement in 1908. In 1890, he published Principles of Economics—almost a decade in the writing—which saw him become the pre-eminent economic figure in Britain.

At Cambridge Marshall helped establish the neoclassical school of economics that sought to bridge the gap between the classicists (whom he believed overemphasized supply-side influences on price) and assorted Continental schools that were focusing more on demand-side influences. Later major works included Industry and Trade (1919) and Money, Credit, and Commerce (1923). However, plagued by ill-health, he never completed a planned revision of his landmark Principles. He died in Cambridge in 1924.

capital

"Capital" is the term for the manmade resources necessary in a production process. Without capital, there would be no economic activity as we recognize it. That is why competition is so fierce to control capital.

Almost every economic enterprise needs a combination of land, labor, capital, and entrepreneurship. Along with hard capital—infrastructure, buildings, and machinery—we also think in terms of financial capital—the wealth accumulated by an individual or a company that allows them to generate an ongoing income.

Capital, then, allows its possessor to get on with doing the things that will make them more money. So we come to the idea of private property. While most of us living in market-based economies accept the need for a certain level of private property, it is not inevitable. Historically, there have been social groups (including a few extant tribes) who operated systems of common ownership, in which everything is shared on a basis of trust borne of long tradition. Alternatively, Karl Marx and his followers espoused collective ownership, with assets utilized so as to best serve society's needs.

Private ownership, however, has been practiced across large swathes of the planet since ancient times. The likes of Aristotle were convinced that common ownership was doomed to failure since no one had an incentive to oversee the efficient use of resources. The prospect of owning private property, by contrast, offers an incentive to work hard and to seek to do things in better and more efficient ways. Without private property, the notion of the market and of commercial competition dissolves and technological development is curbed.

private property brings progress

The Industrial Revolution offers a case study in how private property spurred an advance that has, it is widely accepted, benefited society as a whole. The leading lights of the Industrial Revolution were inspired to create new ways of working— from harnessing steam power and building factories to inventing new means of spinning yarn—because there were financial rewards to be had. Would the same advances have been made if the only reward on offer was the gratitude of fellow citizens reaping the benefit of the industrialists' long hours of labor and leaps of the imagination? It is, we must assume, unlikely.

Yet capitalism (the system which allows private ownership of capital) is far from problem-free, not least because money has a habit of staying in the same hands. When capital is concentrated among a small section of society, individuals outside this elite who may themselves be blessed with prodigious talents and a strong work ethic can be denied access to it. In this way, not only does the individual miss out but society is also deprived of their potential. Indeed, Marx regarded private property as nothing less than the means by which the capitalist can keep the workers in servitude.

Even though Marx seemed to have lost the argument by the end of the 20th century, the turmoil of recent years has resulted in renewed questioning of the unfettered capitalist model.

what are you worth?

Another crucial form of capital is "human capital," the umbrella term for all the know-how, skills, and talents that determine how productive an individual is. If two workers put in exactly the same number of hours at work, the worker with higher human capital will be the more productive. That, in theory, is why skilled workers (workers with higher human capital) get paid more than unskilled workers.

Increasingly, employers have come to realize that investment in human capital is just as important as investment in new buildings or equipment. A well-educated and highly trained staff provides companies with a competitive edge. Consider, for instance, a company that employs two plumbers. Both have identical vans and equipment, and both work 35 hours per week. Employee 1, though, has studied plumbing at college and has several months' practical experience. The company also pays to send him on courses to keep his skills up to date. Employee 2 has been employed as a favor despite never having picked up a plunger in his life. Employee 1 thus gets through far more jobs than his colleague every day and works to a higher standard. Sure, his bosses may be paying more to send him away on training, but their investment is returned many times over.

types of economy

An economy is made up of all the production, trade, and consumption within a given geographical area—be it a neighborhood, a town, a region, a country, even the entire planet. Most economies involve a mixture of activity types. However, geography, demographics, and tradition heavily influence the balance.

Early economies were essentially agricultural. For millennia, most people spent most of their working lives toiling to produce food by growing crops or raising livestock. It was labor-intensive work, and economic activity was largely restricted to trading agricultural produce or the equipment necessary to its production. Today, agriculture is still part of every major economy, but its relative importance has diminished startlingly in developed nations. So, while the U.S. remains a major agricultural producer, agriculture accounts for less than 5% of its total economic activity; the figure for China, meanwhile, is just under 10%. In many less-developed countries, agriculture remains more economically significant. In Ethiopia, for example, the sector accounts for over 45% of the economy.

industry and services

The Industrial Revolution marked a sea change in many economies away from an agricultural base toward an industrial one. Before the Industrial Revolution, a period of technological development in agriculture led to greater efficiency in the sector, freeing up supplies of capital, labor, and entrepreneurism for use in other areas. It also meant people had more money to spend on non-agricultural products. Ever-larger numbers of workers left rural areas to work in factories that made consumer goods and industrial equipment. Britain, home of the Industrial Revolution, was transformed from a largely agricultural economy to a predominantly industrial one. Much of what we term the developed world followed suit, establishing a pattern that lasted well into the 20th century. Many of the emerging economic powerhouses of the present century—most notably China—have similarly used an industrial base (and, in China's case, its huge workforce) to spur growth.

However, after World War II many of the world's strongest economies, the U.S. included, moved from an industrial base to a services one. For the first time in history, the planet's economic giants focused less on growing food and making things than on providing service industries. Today, over half the U.S. working population is employed in the service sector, which encompasses everything from government, banking, and retail to education, hospitality, and the creative industries. According to the CIA *World Fact Book*, all of the top 15 economies in the world today are dominated by the service sector—except China, where it is still the largest single sector despite accounting for less than 50% of all economic activity. While industry and agriculture are vital components of the overall economic picture, we truly live in the age of the services industry. Many economists argue that the shift from an agriculture-dominated economy to an industrial one and then a service-based economy is a tell-tale sign of long-term growth.

the new economy

The "new economy" was a term that gained currency in the 1990s, a time when the great ideological battle between capitalism and communism appeared to have been settled decisively in favor of the former and technological innovations (especially the growth of the IT sector, biotechnology, and the birth of the internet) offered dreams of new economic horizons. For a while at the end of that decade it was enough to jot down a web-based business idea (not necessarily a very good one) and you'd find some hopeful investor throwing money at you, intent on hopping on to the dot.com bandwagon. Everyone wanted to be part of the brave new economy in which hi-tech would drive exponential growth. Of course, things did not work out quite as planned, and many enterprises fell by the wayside as the marketplace became overcrowded and cracks appeared in countless business plans. Nonetheless, the new economy has lived on in all those tech companies (think Microsoft and Apple), internet giants (Google and Amazon), and bio-tech behemoths (the likes of Gilead Sciences and Amgen Inc.) that have prospered at the forefront of hi-tech innovation. Furthermore, their new ways of working and doing business increasingly permeate the wider economy, so that the new economy appears to be more than just a 1990s pipe dream after all.

the Kuznets curve

The Kuznets curve plots per capita income against economic inequality to illustrate Simon Kuznets' hypothesis that industrial growth brings first an increase in economic inequality followed by a sustained decrease.

The relationship between economic growth and equality is a subject of eternal fascination for economists. The Kuznets curve is not the last word on the subject, but it provides a valuable insight into the complex dynamic. The curve was developed by Simon Kuznets in the 1950s and 1960s to support his thesis on how economies grow. He contended that as an economy first industrializes (typically moving from an agricultural base), per capita income rises but a greater proportion of wealth accumulation accrues to those who already hold capital and can seize investment opportunities.

Furthermore, because the early stages of industrialization are typically accompanied by a mass migration of the labor force from the countryside into cities, employers are able to keep wage increases down. In this way, the gap between the rich and poor grows, even as per capita income increases. In addition, as rural communities lose workers to the cities, the wealth gap between urban and rural populations accelerates.

ups and downs

However, over the longer term, wages find their natural (increased) level, while industrialization and urbanization bring about social changes such as improved levels of education and better welfare provision. Improved education produces workers who are more highly skilled and can thus demand higher wages, and individuals become better equipped to innovate and take advantage of new business opportunities, prompting a more profound redistribution of wealth. Welfare provision, meanwhile, provides an institutional structure for the transfer of wealth from the rich to the poor. As a result, overall inequality declines over time.

Critics of the Kuznets curve included Kuznets himself, who acknowledged the "fragility" of the data (gathered from many different countries) on which his work was based. Others have pointed out that certain countries have a historic proclivity toward economic inequality, while other countries industrialize without necessarily exhibiting

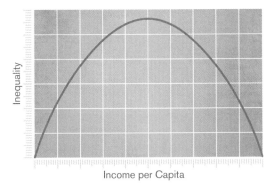

Inequality

Income per Capita

the characteristics of the curve. Economists Alberto Alesina and Dani Rodrik, Italian and Turkish respectively, took a very different view of the relationship between economic growth and equality in their joint paper of 1994, "Distributive Politics and Economic Growth." They inverted the question of how growth impacts equality to ask how equality impacts growth. They concluded that more equal societies grow more quickly, in part because societies with greater wealth disparity are more likely to have a higher tax rate on accumulated wealth (as demanded by the less wealthy majority), which, they contend, is a natural disincentive to pursue economic expansion.

In recent years, the Kuznets curve has enjoyed a further, somewhat unexpected, lease of life in the form of the environmental Kuznets curve, which plots per capita income against environmental degradation.

Simon Kuznets

Simon Kuznets was born in 1901 in Pinsk in what was then the Russian Empire and is now Belarus. He undertook studies at the Kharkiv Institute of Commerce from 1918, but civil war led to his relocating to the U.S. in 1922. He received his BSc from Columbia University in 1923, a masters a year later, and a doctorate in 1926. From 1927 until 1961, he worked at the National Bureau of Economic Research, where he was instrumental in establishing international standards for national-income accounting. He also held a series of academic posts, variously at the University of Pennsylvania, Johns Hopkins University, and Harvard. During World War II he was posted to the Bureau of Planning and Statistics and after the war served as advisor to governments around the world. In 1947, he cofounded the International Association for Research and was later president of both the American Statistical Association (1949) and the American Economic Association (1954). His published works included *National Income and Its Composition, 1919–1938* (1941), *Modern Economic Growth: Rate, Structure, and Spread* (1967), and *Economic Growth of Nations: Total Output and Production Structure* (1971).

He was awarded the Nobel Prize in 1971 for "his empirically founded interpretation of economic growth which has led to new and deepened insight into the economic and social structure and process of development." He died in Cambridge, Massachusetts, in 1985.

sustainable growth

Growth, in economic terms, is an economy's increased capacity to produce goods and services. It is the goal that drives the economic policy of governments around the globe. But is it a realistic one?

With a few notable exceptions, most economists see growth as not only the most important sign that an economy is healthy but as the key to improving quality of life. Given that every year there are more people on the planet who need to be catered for, there is great pressure to maintain growth.

The Holy Grail is for sustainable growth—that is, incremental growth over a long period, achieved in a way that does not imperil the prospects of future generations. It is all well and good for an economy to grow by 10% one year, but meaningless if it declines by that amount or more the next. Economic growth that fluctuates from year to year breeds uncertainty. What if this year turns out to be a bad one? Will I lose my job? Should I spend less and save more? Should the government cut back on its spending programs? Uncertainty makes everybody nervous and scares off investors so that an economy's longer-term outlook goes into decline.

slow and steady

It is far better to grow at a reasonable rate, year on year, because even a modest annual increment has a major impact over a longer period. If, for instance, an economy grows by 2.5% per annum, the entire economy will double in size within three decades—an impressive feat by anyone's standards.

There are many ways to measure growth (see "Measuring the Economy," page 110) but one key comparison is between growth across an economy as a whole and on a per capita basis (calculated by dividing the figure for the total economy by the population size). Many economists believe the second measure is a far more useful indicator. This is because there are two main spurs to economic growth:

- **A greater volume of inputs, especially capital and labor. More is produced simply because more is put into the production process. For instance, a factory may reasonably expect to increase its output if it increases the number of workers by 10%.**

is zero growth such a bad thing?

While most economists hold with the orthodoxy that growth is good, there are some dissenters. What, they ask, has over two centuries of fairly consistent, post-Industrial Revolution global growth actually done for us? Yes, those of us lucky to live in the developed world boast lots of material benefits and have more leisure time than any previous generation in human history. Yet poverty is rife across swathes of the globe, many natural resources are stretched to breaking point, and we face the prospect of an environmental Armageddon. In recent years, a school of economic thought has emerged that argues we would be better served by aiming for zero growth instead—in which economies do not expand at all but remain in a state of equilibrium. The quality of life may go down in certain respects, they concede, but that is a sacrifice worth making if it means we preserve natural resources and slow down the industrial impact on environmental degradation. We might not have everything we want, but we will still have a planet to live on, the zero-growthers (and the even more extreme de-growthers) argue. Furthermore, they say, it will force us away from an economic model that inherently causes economic inequality. But zero-growth opponents remain unconvinced. For starters, even if zero growth might be sustainable in the world's richest countries (and the jury is out on that one), it is certainly not in poorer nations already struggling to meet basic living standards. In any case, they claim, the market economy left to its own devices will protect scarce resources by setting a high price point, while the market will prompt innovation that addresses the environmental threat.

can you keep your house in order?

If you want to get a sense of how the economy as a whole is performing, you can do a lot worse than keep an eye on the property market. The housing market tends to be relatively stable over the medium to long term, so that a stagnation or decline is considered a concrete indicator of trouble in the wider economy. In a boom time, when jobs are plentiful and incomes thriving, more people feel confident to enter the housing market. In turn, house prices rise and investors finance new properties to meet demand. New jobs are created, adding to the economic good feeling until prices rise too high. Investment in new building falls, affecting not only the construction industry but all those subsidiary industries attached to it. Furthermore, homeowners tend to get very jumpy if they think their property–probably the single biggest investment most of us make–is about to lose value and will often decide the time has come to tighten their belts. So begins the descent from boom to bust. There are those who suggest that the building of skyscrapers has an even more direct correlation to the cycle of boom and bust. The Empire State Building in New York opened just in time for the Wall Street Crash, for instance, while the Petronas Towers in Kuala Lumpar neatly presaged the 1997 Asian financial crisis. As Barclays Capital put it in 2012, skyscrapers often represent "a widespread misallocation of capital and an impending economic correction."

- **More efficient use of inputs. Growth occurs without additional inputs when technological innovation allows existing inputs to be used better. The same factory, for example, may increase its yield by 10% if the labor force has access to training and equipment that allows it to work 10% more efficiently.**

The per capita measure better indicates whether an economy has potential for sustainable growth because it shows whether or not the productivity of each individual is increasing. On the other hand, a rise in an economy's overall size may simply come down to there being more people in it, which ultimately puts additional strain on scarce resources. Also, when businesses work smarter—so the theory goes—individuals get richer, the workforce has more leisure time, and there is greater opportunity for education, which, in turn, leads to more innovation, allowing the cycle of growth to continue.

boom and bust

We described sustainable growth as the Holy Grail because it is elusive and no one knows for sure if it really exists. As yet, no economy has achieved it, succumbing instead to the vicissitudes of the boom-and-bust cycle.

While Adam Smith described a model of the economy in which the forces of the market ensure long-term balance, it was clear to other economists that this idea of equilibrium was illusory. In the early 19th century, Jean-Charles Sismondi, a Swiss historian, highlighted that economies are subject to regular disturbances, while in the 1820s Frenchman Charles Dunoyer wrote of the cyclical nature of the economy, describing how it swings between periods of heightened economic activity (boom) and downturns (bust). This cycle is sometimes called the business cycle.

It is widely argued that a bust occurs when production outpaces consumption. In boom times, success begets success. As the economy thrives, the labor force expands, workers are paid more and consume more, raising demand that fuels further economic activity. However, as producers fight for market share, they increase production until it outstrips demand. This causes prices to drop, leading employers to cut wages and lay workers off, so reducing the size of the market. Consumption falls further, prompting increasing nervousness among investors, leading to further reductions in wages and layoffs. So the economy goes into a tailspin. Only when prices are driven down far enough does demand pick up again, and the road back to Boomville opens up.

boom and bust is natural

Until Sismondi and Dunoyer identifed the business cycle, busts tended to be blamed on extraordinary events such as wars or natural disasters. Subsequently, economists began to view the boom-and-bust cycle as a naturally occurring phenomenon—not

that it has stopped leaders and politicians the world over from searching for a way to short-circuit the cycle.

One such figure, who notoriously fell foul of the belief that he could hold back the economic tide like a modern-day Cnut, was Gordon Brown, Chancellor of the Exchequer of the UK from 1997 to 2008. Take, for instance, a speech he made shortly after coming to office in May 1997:

> **Stability is necessary for our future economic success. The British economy of the future must be built not on the shifting sands of boom and bust, but on the bedrock of prudent and wise economic management for the long term.**

It was a message that Brown reiterated many times over the following years, and it looked as if he might just have succeeded, as the British economy enjoyed an unprecedented decade of growth. By 2008, however, the economy, and that of the world at large, was entering the doldrums, and Brown conceded that he was powerless to do much about it, commenting that "if you go around the world, you will see that every country is affected."

Economics strives to make the unpredictable predictable. While we cannot necessarily plot the pattern of boom and bust (although economists are constantly striving to do so), we can be sure that good times will follow bad, just as bad times will follow good.

creative destruction

Joseph Schumpeter believed that innovation, characterized by the entrepreneur, is the key to economic progress. He therefore took an untypically upbeat view of recessions, arguing they eliminate inefficient players from the market and make space for growth.

In his seminal work *Capitalism, Socialism and Democracy* (1942) Schumpeter argued that "the process of creative destruction is the essential fact about capitalism." But what did he mean by "creative destruction"? Essentially, that innovation leads to the death of old economic structures and the birth of new ones.

History offers numerous examples of creative destruction. Most obvious, perhaps, is the Industrial Revolution, where innovations such as the steam engine and the beginnings of mass production did away with older, less efficient ways of doing business. In more recent times, we might look at the way the creation of digital audio files revolutionized the music industry or how internet news is supplanting the traditional newspaper business.

Schumpeter derived the concept of creative destruction from the work of Karl Marx (see page 66). Marx believed that the inherent need of capitalism to reconfigure the economic order and devalue existing wealth in order to create new wealth brought about a cycle of socially divisive crises that would ultimately destroy capitalism itself. Schumpeter, by contrast, believed creative destruction was a vital component of human progress and brought living standards up. Furthermore, he saw crises, such as recessions, as instrumental in the process, clearing the pitch of the old and outmoded in favor of the new and fresh. In other words, the failing companies, collapsing industries, and unemployment that we associate with economic downturns are all essential stepping stones on the road to progress.

thinking differently

Schumpeter also made it clear that creative destruction is not driven by technological innovation (new inventions and products) alone but by the introduction of new types of commercial models and modes of production and different ways of doing business. Where Adam Smith saw capital as the driver of capitalism, and for Marx it was the exploitation of workers, Schumpeter was convinced it was entrepreneurs, every bit as much as inventors, who, by introducing new ideas, create new markets.

He also contended that entrepreneurism thrives best in a monopolistic environment rather than in the perfect market (in which all agents theoretically produce the same goods and access the same technology), since the desire to achieve and then maintain a monopoly forces the monopoly to innovate constantly or else succumb to somebody else's new idea. Nonetheless, he also acknowledged the propensity for monopolies to become overly bureaucratic and inefficient.

Like Marx (but with considerably less relish) Schumpeter argued that creative destruction would ultimately lead to the collapse of capitalism. But, while Marx argued this was because of the system's inherent failures, Schumpeter believed capitalism's successes contained the kernel of its downfall by removing the institutional structures needed to prop it up. For instance, he suspected that capitalism would lead to the creation of an expanded intellectual class that attacked the very bourgeois principles that birthed it. This was the pay-off of the "process of industrial mutation that incessantly revolutionizes the economic structure from within, incessantly destroying the old one, incessantly creating a new one."

Joseph Schumpeter

Joseph Schumpeter was born in Triesch in Moravia (then part of the Austro-Hungarian Empire, now in the Czech Republic) in 1883. His father, a factory owner, died when he was four, and the family moved to Vienna. He studied law at the University of Vienna, earning his doctorate in 1906, and in 1907 he married Gladys Seaver, whom he would divorce in 1913. In 1909, he was made a professor of economics and politics at the University of Czernowitz, and in 1911 he took up a new posting at the University of Graz. After World War I, he was minister of finance in the short-lived Republic of German Austria. In 1921 he became president of the Biedermann Bank but resigned five years later when it was taken over. He married again in 1925, to Anna Reisinger, who died in childbirth the following year. By then he had resumed academic life at the University of Bonn, but with the rise of European fascism he moved to the U.S. in 1932. There he lectured at Harvard, and, in 1937, he married for the third and final time, to the American economic historian Elizabeth Boody. That same year, he published *The Theory of Economic Development.* Two years later he took U.S. citizenship and published *Business Cycles.* His most famous work, *Capitalism, Socialism and Democracy,* followed in 1945. He died in Taconic, Connecticut, in 1950. His widow posthumously published his *History of Economic Analysis* in 1954.

economic
bubbles

Closely linked to the boom-and-bust cycle is the concept of the economic bubble, in which the value of an asset rises in an unsustainable fashion, sometimes seemingly by force of will alone. The impact of a bubble bursting can be devastating.

A "bubble" is the term used to describe the cumulative price in the rise of an asset, driven principally by the belief that the price will rise further. People keep investing in an asset simply because they are convinced that they will be able to sell at a profit, even if other indicators might suggest the asset has reached its optimum value. When the bubble bursts—demand for the asset crashes—those who invested in it at an elevated price are at risk of large losses.

Economic bubbles can seem like a bout of collective madness, but, however guarded we may be, they recur with unnerving regularity. The global crash that began in 2008 stemmed from the bubble popping in the U.S. property market in 2007. For years, financial institutions agreed to provide unsuitable mortgages to high-risk buyers (the fabled subprime mortgages), who themselves were unduly confident that they would be able to repay their mortgages thanks to the apparently inexorable rise of property prices. Lenders and borrowers alike engaged in a mortgage frenzy until the bubble burst as demand dipped and doubts were raised about the security of many of the loans. As a result, house prices collapsed, borrowers were unable to meet their mortgage payments, and lenders foreclosed (i.e., repossessed properties), writing off billions in bad debt. The impact, of course, was felt across the U.S. and the international economy for years to come.

lessons not learned

Prior to that was the dot.com bubble of the late 1990s. Vast sums were invested in internet businesses that often had little chance of long-term success. A heady combination of an emerging technology, a media frenzy for all things web, and often ill-informed investors terrified of missing out ensured that a temporary insanity took hold. When the bubble burst in the early 2000s, many fortunes had been lost as investors slowly began to get to grips with the reality of what cyberspace might offer and how we as a society could make use of it.

what are bull and bear markets?

Much as we hope that the actions of markets are dictated by logic and restraint, there is no denying that they have their own momentum. In the rush to maximize profits or minimize losses, traders are wont to follow the herd without necessarily assessing each trade on its merits. So we end up with the extremes of bull and bear markets, the former associated with periods of boom and the latter with bust. A bull market is one in which optimism reigns. Investors pour money in, confident that they will be able to ship their holdings on for a profit in the future, so sending the price of assets rising higher still and reeling in more investors keen to make a fast buck. Should the wider economy begin to stutter, suddenly those stock prices start to fall, and previously confident investors look to ship stock before they incur too many losses, driving the price further down. New investors are put off by the reduced opportunity to make a profit—and the market goes into a nose dive. This is called a bear market. It is telling that Wall Street is adorned with a sculpture of a bull, the work of Italian-American artist Arturo Di Modica. Traders would do well to remember that a bull out of control is a dangerous thing.

flower power

Economic bubbles are not just a feature of modern life. One of the first to be documented was the Dutch tulip craze of the 1630s. Such was the desire for the flower that a single bulb could sell for the price of a house before the mania lifted and prices fell until a tulip fetched about the same as an onion. The Dutch economy took years to recover from this dark episode. Seemingly, the wider world failed to heed the warning.

wealth

Most people have a desire to achieve a level of wealth that allows them to live at least comfortably. But just what do we mean when we talk about wealth? Do you consider yourself wealthy?

Technically, wealth is the measure of the net market value of all the assets (tangible and intangible) owned by an individual, social group, organization, or country, less any debts and liabilities. It is distinct from income, which is a measure of money or other assets (a salary, say, or interest on investments) received over a given period, independent of capital holdings. The assets considered when measuring wealth include monies, real estate, valuables (such as works of art), shareholdings, and intellectual property (including trademarks and patents). Some measures of wealth also take account of prospective assets, including pensions and likely inheritances. So how much is enough to classify one as wealthy?

Although, as already mentioned, wealth and income are not the same, the latter can offer a good indication of the former. In 2012, the International Labour Organization figured out that the world's average wage was PPP$1,480 per month (PPP$17,760 per year). They used PPP (Purchasing Power Parity) dollars to take account of the fact that there is great variance between countries as to what an actual dollar will buy you. Using PPP dollars allows a sensible comparison of earnings by looking at what a given income will allow you to purchase in any given country. So if you have an income above PPP$18,000 per year, you may well consider yourself to be toward the upper half of the wealth spectrum.

does money buy you happiness?

However, to enter the realms of the super-wealthy, you need assets valued in the billions of dollars. In 2015, *Forbes* magazine (that great chronicle of wealth) reported that the number of billionaires around the world had reached a record 1,826, with an aggregate net worth of $7.05 trillion. The U.S. contributed a greater number by far than any other nation, accounting for about 30% of the total. Next came China, whose 12% contribution was more than double that of the third-placed nation, Germany.

The ultimate million-dollar-question is whether being wealthy also makes you happy. In 2015, an intriguing report was published in the academic journal *Social Psychological and Personality Science*. A team of psychologists and behavioral scientists from Michigan State University and the University of British Columbia used census data for almost 13,000 people to study the links between income and reported happiness levels. They found that, while the better-off were not necessarily happier for having more money, their ability to access money to deal with crisis situations (such as a leaking roof) meant they were less sad than the poorer subjects, concluding:

We show that higher income is associated with experiencing less daily sadness but has no bearing on daily happiness.

That 18th-century behemoth of American civilization Benjamin Franklin was more skeptical that wealth can buy you happiness:

Money never made a man happy yet, nor will it. There is nothing in its nature to produce happiness. The more a man has, the more he wants. Instead of filling a vacuum, it makes one.

how rich is rich?

It is a thankless task to try to calculate the richest man in history given the difficulties in retrospectively assessing a subject's assets, not to mention the impact of inflation and exchange rates measured over millennia. Nonetheless, some have tried, with the Celebrity Net Worth website plumping for the little-known Mansa Musa I, a 14th-century ruler of the Malian Empire, whose wealth in modern terms they put at $400 billion.

There is a strong argument, though, that the American industrialist and oil baron John D. Rockefeller is the wealthiest self-made man in history. As boss of the Standard Oil Company, by the early 20th century he had a 90% share of the global oil-refinery business. At its peak, his wealth was equivalent to about 1.5% of the total GDP of the U.S. That is some three times the rate of Bill Gates, the current richest man in the world.

On Rockefeller's death in 1937, *The New York Times* estimated he had earned $1.5 billion over his lifetime. Adjusted for inflation, it is thought that he boasted a fortune of some $340 billion at current prices. Notoriously ruthless in accumulating his wealth, he went on to become arguably the greatest philanthropist of his age, which suggests that he perhaps gained as much satisfaction from giving his wealth away as he did from building it up.

how can the wealthy affect redistribution?

According to the World Bank, in 2011 just over a billion people were living on less than the bank's designated poverty line of $1.25 per day. Meanwhile, Bill Gates, the world's richest man (and one of the world's foremost philanthropists, see page 104), had an estimated fortune of $81.2 billion as of January 2015 (which makes him the richest man in history in dollar terms). To put that in perspective, only about a third of the world's countries boasted GDPs for 2014 worth more than Gates. But, in recent years, Gates has been a major player in wealth redistribution. The Bill and Melinda Gates Foundation makes philanthropic grants equivalent to about 10% of the entire U.S. aid budget, and Gates himself has vowed to give over 95% of his personal wealth to the foundation. Perhaps the most noteworthy achievement of the foundation so far is its role in the almost complete eradication of polio, which as recently as 1988 left some 350,000 people a year (mostly children) paralyzed. As Gates noted in 2013: "Polio's pretty special because once you get an eradication you no longer have to spend money on it; it's just there as a gift for the rest of time." That is money truly well spent.

wealth distribution

A healthy economy is one that is not only wealthy but which shares the wealth as widely and equitably as possible. The study of wealth distribution compares and analyzes how wealth is distributed among individuals and different segments of a society. It is widely accepted that a fair and wide distribution is necessary not only for social welfare and justice, but for long-term economic prosperity to be sustained.

If, for instance, wealth is concentrated in the hands of a small number of people, there is a natural cap on the market. Consumption is artificially constrained (even the greediest individual has limits as to what they want and need) which, in turn, curbs competition in the market and thus the incentive to experiment and innovate. We know that economies struggle to grow in a healthy way without technological innovation. In fact, increasing levels of wealth inequality are considered a marker of impending recession.

rich world, poor world

Despite hard evidence that wide and fair distribution of wealth is good for us all, the raw data does not always make for easy reading. Indeed, there are clear indicators that we are living in an era in which things are heading the wrong way. For example, according to Credit Suisse's annual Global Wealth Report for 2014, the poorest half of the global population owns less than 1% of total wealth, and the richest 1% hold 48.2% of global assets. Meanwhile, the charity Oxfam has reported that the world's richest 85 individuals owned wealth equivalent to the world's poorest 3.5 billion people.

There are clear global discrepancies, too. The same Credit Suisse report reveals that North America claims some 35% of global wealth but only a little over 5% of the population, while Africa, with almost 12% of the population, has only about 1% of the wealth.

Inequality does not exist only between regions and states. Take the world's largest economy, the U.S. In 2014, *Fortune* magazine reported the findings of economists Emmanuel Saez and Gabriel Zucman. They claim that in the late 1970s the wealthiest 0.1% of American families earned about 7% of total income but that by 2012 the figure had more than tripled to 22%. Indeed, it was ominously back to levels not seen since the era of the Great Depression. After that cataclysmic economic collapse of the 1920s and 1930s came some four decades of wealth democratization before the trend went into a startling reverse that the U.S.'s recent economic travails have done little to stem.

Wealth inequality is not only bad for business but encourages a culture of bad credit, cuts opportunities for social mobility, and seriously endangers social cohesion. Addressing the problem promises to be one of the great economic challenges of this age.

accounting

From a powerful finance minister to the small business owner or wage-earner supporting a family, it pays to know what money you have coming in and what is going out.

An account is a written record of economic activity over a given time span. Most of us are familiar with statements of account from our banks, detailing our various financial transactions (deposits, credits, withdrawals, etc.) on a monthly basis. While accounts don't need be intrinsically complicated, they often are, which is why professional accountants are powerful figures in our society.

When it comes to business accounting, there are two broad branches. Management accounting presents relevant data to owners and managers to provide a full picture of their business's economic health, enabling them to make informed decisions on their future. Financial accounting summarizes a business's activities for third-party consumption, including tax offices, banks, and potential investors. (Bear in mind that tax accounts use the "tax year," which varies from country to country and often does not correlate to the calendar year.) Financial accounting is governed by protocols set out in the Generally Accepted Accounting Principle (GAAP).

the numbers game

Business accounts are of three main types:

- A profit-and-loss account details all the monies coming into and going out of an enterprise over a given period (typically a month, a quarter, or a year), with profit or loss (the bottom line) calculated by subtracting outgoings from income.
- A balance sheet serves as a snapshot of a company's health at a given moment in time. It lists the monetary values of all assets (everything a company owns to run its business) and its liabilities (debts). Key to the balance sheet is the following equation:

$$assets = liabilities + equity$$

Equity here relates to any claims a company's owners have on the company's assets (the size of the claim in proportion to the size of their holding in the business). The balance sheet always balances because any excess left after liabilities have been subtracted from assets is listed as equity.

The worth of the business is, however, much greater than the value of the assets as compared with the liabilities. A negative figure indicates a business that is technically insolvent, meaning its assets are worth less than the full extent of its liabilities. However, even a technically insolvent company can carry on trading if it has sufficient working capital (i.e. capital that is not tied up in real estate or fixed assets) to pay its immediate debts (bills and wages, for example). This information is contained in the third main type of account, the cashflow statement.

Governments also have to keep their accounts in order—no easy task considering the amount of economic activity across an entire country. Most importantly, national accounts show whether a country is running a deficit or a surplus (whether the country is in debt or not). But the government account we tend to show most interest in is the annual budget, which sets out the expected incomes and outlays for the year ahead—and gives us a good idea as to whether we will be paying more or less tax.

who's been cooking the books?

Accountancy has a long and respected pedigree. However, the profession was put through the wringer at the start of the 21st century amid a plethora of high-profile accounting scandals. Most infamous was the collapse in 2001 of Houston-based energy company Enron. With annual revenues exceeding $100 billion per year, Enron was a seriously big business. When it was found that the company had misrepresented its finances, hiding away billions of dollars of debt, the company was forced to file for bankruptcy—the largest corporate bankruptcy in U.S. history at the time. Several executives, including its founder Kenneth Lay, were subsequently convicted of fraud. Their crimes were committed even as the company's accounts were being audited by Arthur Andersen, one of the world's "Big Five" auditing firms. That they could have failed to arrest the wayward activities of some Enron employees led to a crisis of faith in accounting practices, compounded in 2002 by the bankruptcy of WorldCom (which stole the crown as America's largest bankruptcy from Enron), and effectively ended Andersen's long history as a leading accounting firm. Luca Pacioli, the great Renaissance mathematician who revolutionized accountancy by introducing the concept of double-entry bookkeeping, must have been spinning in his grave.

forecasting

Economists aim to learn the lessons
of yesterday in order to create a better
tomorrow. But how do they go about it?

Every economic decision is based on an
evaluation of what is likely to result from
taking a certain course of action. Although
the future is unpredictable, economists have
an array of strategies to help their forecasts.

reading the signs

One technique uses extrapolation, which
means studying existing data and trends
and extending them into the future. To this
end, economists may employ time-series
data, which detail fluctuations in the same
economic variable at specified time intervals.
For instance, if oil prices have been rising
for four years, it may be reasonable to
assume that they will continue to do so.
However, if a survey of a century's worth of
data shows that oil prices consistently rose in
four-year cycles before falling for a year, it

may be possible to extrapolate an imminent
decline in oil prices. Extrapolation relies on
expert reading of past trends and assumes
that life is a preplotted line on a graph—
something experience tells us is not true.

Another method involves the study of
leading indicators—economic factors that
tend to change ahead of wider changes
in the economy. For instance, falling
house prices suggest imminent economic
contraction. The general economic climate
can also be assessed from survey data taken
from individuals and businesses about their
economic plans at a given time. Such data
will typically be gathered by government
organizations, market-research companies,
and private commercial operations.

Then there is the economic model—a
theoretical construct that reflects the real-
world economy so that a hypothesis can be
tested within it. Since economies are subject
to a complex amalgam of influences and
effectors, an economic model attempts to
mirror all relevant constants and show how
a particular course of action will impact
on as many of the variables as possible.
The results may be both quantitative and
qualitative. The discipline was significantly
advanced in the 1930s by Norwegian
economist Ragnar Frisch, who developed a
system of econometrics, using mathematical
and statistical analysis to prove or disprove
particular hypotheses. Nonetheless,
the fundamental problem of economic
modeling persists—our inability to take
account of all the possible variables.

how can you miss a global collapse?

With the fall of communism in the Soviet Union and Eastern Europe by the early 1990s, there was a sense that the Western liberal-capitalist model had prevailed. The political economist Francis Fukuyama went so far as to ponder whether we had reached "the end of history."

It now seems likely that such speculation engendered a certain complacency in our economists (although, it must be said, they were hardly the only ones to succumb to a little self-congratulation). But it was not long before evidence emerged of a collective failure to keep one's eye on the ball. By 2007, it was evident that the U.S. housing market was in serious difficulty, thanks to the rapid expansion of the subprime mortgage business. Financial institutions found themselves dangerously exposed having spent years dealing in increasingly complex financial products that it turned out very few people really understood. A long period of prosperity had created a sense that the party would never end. Certainly, there were few experts willing to be cast as the party pooper. This led to what a group of leading British economists in 2009 called a "failure of the collective imagination." There had been a few dissenting voices, of course, such as analyst Peter Schliff, who in 2006 wrote of seeing a "real financial crisis coming," but his was little more than a voice in the wilderness in an episode that cast the art of economic forecasting in a very dim light.

As the writer and philosopher George Santayana famously put it: "Those who cannot remember the past are condemned to repeat it."

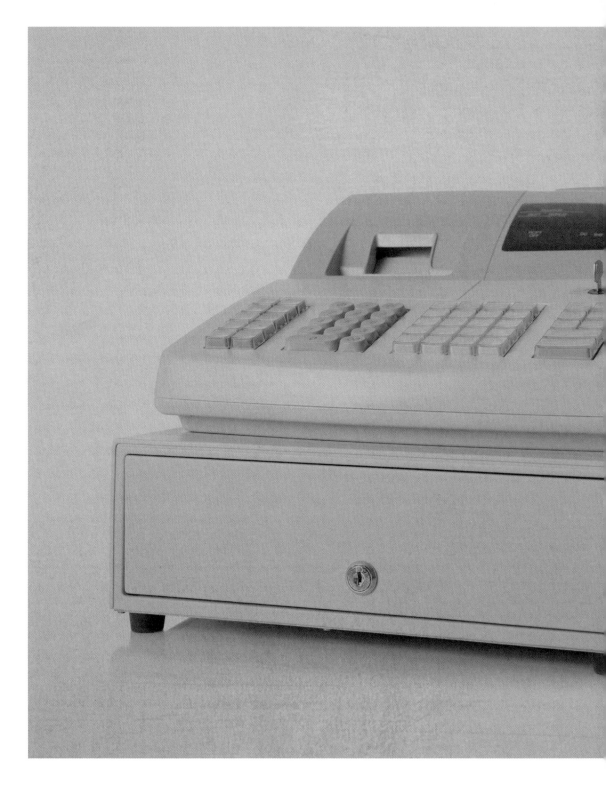

how does commerce work?

give & take

to interfere or not

in it to win it

Marxian economics

less for more

big is better

game theory

getting down to business

keeping order

knowledge is power

Pareto efficiency

3

give & take

At the heart of the market is the concept of supply and demand. The market continually strives for the perfect balance between the volume of goods and services that consumers demand and the volume that suppliers provide.

So many factors can affect the relationship between supply and demand, but at its most basic, demand relates to the amount of a good or service that consumers want at a certain price, while supply relates to the quantity of a good or service that producers make available at a given price.

Consumers and suppliers both face two fundamental questions in the marketplace:

- **The consumer must first decide whether they want a product and then whether they are prepared to pay the price being demanded. The first question is often the simplest. Imagine you are in front of a stall selling cups of hot coffee and another** selling mugs of cold mud. It is a fair bet that you'll want to buy from the first trader and ignore the other. The second question is harder. Are you prepared to spend your money on a coffee, or would you rather save it for something else? Would your decision be different if a coffee was cheaper? "What do I want?" and "How much do I want it?" are the two factors that determine demand.

- **The supplier has different but related questions to ponder. First, "Is there demand for what I intend to provide?" Trader one has thought about likely demand when deciding to sell coffee, while his rival has not! Second, "How much to charge?" To maximize profit the trader has to work out the price most people will pay. If the price is not more than it costs the supplier to provide then they won't be in business for long.**

price matters but isn't everything

The consumer's decision can be influenced by external factors. Are they wearing a new outfit that they don't want to risk spilling coffee down? Has there just been a health scare about caffeine intake? The supplier, on the other hand, might find that drought in Kenya ruins the crop, forcing up the cost of beans. Perhaps demand spikes with the onset of an unexpected cold snap. Or a local office relocates, removing half the customer base at a stroke. All these imponderables can seriously impact on supply and demand.

what is equilibrium?

The general law of supply and demand is simple: if all other factors remain the same, the lower the price of a good or service, the more consumers will demand it. Conversely, as demand grows, suppliers seek to provide more and at a greater price, thus maximizing their profit. These graphs show how supply and demand curves are inversely proportional to each other. In Graph A, demand declines as price increases, while in B, supply increases in proportion to price rise. Graph C shows the exact point at which the supply and demand curves cross. At this point, the economy is in equilibrium, because the supply of a good or service is precisely equal to the volume being demanded. The extent to which demand or supply moves because of a change in price is known as elasticity. The bigger the change, the more elastic it is said to be. In general, the more essential a product the less elastic it is, as consumers have little option but to keep on buying it. So a staple of life, say bread or petrol, will normally be less elastic than a luxury good such as a sports car.

Market equilibrium is the Holy Grail for economists, but, in truth, there are so many factors at play in supply and demand beyond price alone that equilibrium is rarely achieved.

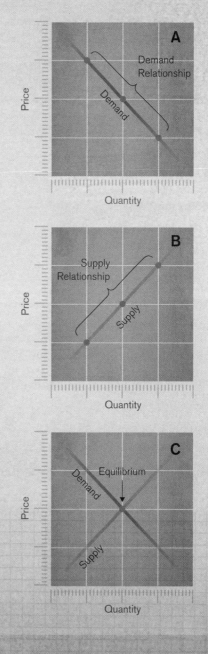

to interfere or not?

John Stuart Mill built on the earlier work of Adam Smith and David Ricardo to create a broad-ranging economic philosophy. Some of his most influential work concerns the relationship between laissez-faire (the free market) and government intervention.

John Stuart Mill's *Principles of Political Economy* (often known simply as *Principles*) first appeared in 1848 and underwent several revisions until a seventh and final edition was published in 1871. It is a formidably wide-ranging work, dealing with subjects as diverse as the nature of labor, the distribution of wealth, the functioning of markets, the relationship between money and value, and the links between economic and social progress.

It is indicative of the enormous scope of *Principles* that the question of government intervention or laissez-faire is not addressed until the fifth volume. In that volume he established the concept of the necessary and optional functions of government. The necessary functions, for Mill, are those habitually practiced by governments without objection, while all other functions are optional and lack universal acceptance, rendering them open to debate.

Mill spent little time arguing against what he regarded as the necessary functions of government, such as minting money, exacting taxes, enforcing property rights, and providing essential public goods and services. In other words, he acknowledged a rightful place for state intervention in the economy. However, while making that admission, he restated his fundamental trust in laissez-faire—in other words, that the market ought to be left to decide economic outcomes unless there is clear reason not to allow it. As he put it, any digression from laissez-faire "unless required by some great good, is a certain evil."

some great good

Just like Smith (but not all of his disciples), Mill sought to define a number of clear examples where the interests of "some great good" are best served by government intervention. Among those qualifying fields were education, environmental protection (an area in which he was far ahead of his time), public charity, regulation of utilities, consumer protection, and the enforcement (or not) of marriage contracts.

Mill, then, was a decidedly pragmatic economist who acknowledged both the underlying strengths of the free market but also its failings. By championing the market while explicitly stating (often for the first time in academic literature) a good many of its shortcomings, he laid the philosophical groundwork for everything from the modern welfare state to divorce law and environmental regulation.

These were, ultimately, in the interests of adapting free-market capitalism so that it more fully met the needs of society. His belief in free markets with a little tweaking around the edges on the part of government helped establish a framework for the kind of mixed economies that drive most people's lives' today. And while Mill did not always have the answers, he elucidated many of the most crucial questions that still occupy economists. Until well into the 20th century, *Principles* served as the set text for students of economics at universities around the world, and it remains an essential read for serious students of the discipline.

John Stuart Mill

John Stuart Mill was born in London in 1806. His father, James Mill, was a philosopher, and from a young age Mill was also influenced by one of his father's friends, Jeremy Bentham, and his theory of utilitarianism ("the greatest good of the greatest number"). Mill Jr. joined the East India Company as a 16-year-old and remained with the company for three decades. In his spare time he wrote extensively on philosophical subjects, espousing personal liberty and utilitarian ideals. He was also a trailblazer in encouraging vigorous scientific and empirical approaches in the fields of political and economic analysis.

Three years after *Principles* was published, Mill married Harriet Taylor, in 1851. Together they worked on several philosophical treatises, including *On Liberty,* arguably Mill's most famous work, which appeared in 1858. That same year, Mill found himself unemployed when the East India Company was dissolved following the Indian Mutiny.

After a sojourn to France, Mill returned to Britain and became the member of parliament for Westminster in 1865. He earned a reputation for radicalism on account of his support for Irish land reform, women's rights, family planning, and education for all. When he failed to win reelection in 1868, he returned to France, spending the rest of his life between London and Avignon. He died in 1873.

in it to win it

Gordon Gekko, fictional antihero of the 1987 movie *Wall Street*, claimed: "greed, for lack of a better word, is good. Greed is right. Greed works." When it comes to commercial enterprises, was he right?

A business makes a profit when revenues exceed costs. If costs outstrip revenues, a loss is made. Most economists agree that businesses are united by a desire to maximize profits, even if not everyone has it as their primary aim at the expense of other considerations. Some have nobler reasons to be in business: because they love to practice a certain trade, they spot a gap in the market, or they want to make a positive contribution to the world. However, once these reasons are met, a business will do all it can to turn a profit. This applies equally to social enterprises, non-profit organizations (they invest profits back into their enterprise), hedge funds, and supermarkets—all business is driven by a profit motive.

boosting the bottom line

Some people find this fact rather distasteful, but is it really? In theory, a profit indicates that the consumer values the good or service being offered at a higher price than it cost to produce it. That the seller has succeeded in adding value in this way is ostensibly something to be lauded. To increase profits, a seller must do one or more of the following: sell more of their product, sell each unit at a higher price, or reduce costs. A hike in sales volume or price might be achieved by, for instance, undertaking an advertising campaign or offering special deals. Often, though, companies take more direct control over costs—for instance, by cutting the workforce to save on wages, or relocating offices to reduce rent, or striking better deals with suppliers. Such approaches can have a startling impact on profits.

Of course, not all businesses pursue profit in a particularly admirable way. They may exploit a lack of competition to hold consumers to ransom, especially if they are selling a non-luxury good. Imagine a village that has been cut off by floods. No transport can reach it, and only one store has any bread left. That store may decide to raise the price of bread in the knowledge that the villagers have little choice but to pay it or go without. Alternatively, some less scrupulous firms seek to maximize profits by cutting costs through suspect strategies such as paying below an accepted minimum wage or using substandard raw materials.

what is the real bottom line?

There are two distinct ways to calculate profits or losses, one of which is favored by accountants and the other by economists. Both methods use the same basic equation (profit/loss = revenue minus costs) but consider costs in very different ways. Accounting profits record only those costs incurred in running the business. For instance, an artisan bakery's costs might include staff wages, the cost of ingredients, rent/mortgage payments, the cost of machinery, plus the cost of running a delivery van. However, economic profits also take into consideration the opportunity costs involved. For example, what if the bakery owner gave up a lucrative banking job to pursue his love of baked goods? If the bakery has costs of $35,000 per year and revenues of $65,000, the accounting profit is $30,000. But if the baker has forgone $50,000 that he earned in his previous job (the opportunity cost), the bakery is actually running an economic loss of $20,000 (revenue of $65,000 minus running costs of $35,000 plus opportunity cost of $50,000).

Accounting profits are of interest to the bank manager, taxman, and the like, but the baker himself gets a far better indication of how his life and finances are going to alter as a result of his career change by looking at the economic profits. Similarly, economists favor economic profits to gain a fuller picture of the true costs and benefits of a particular decision.

Marxian economics

Karl Marx's philosophy inextricably bound economics, politics, and history together. Believing economics to be the driving force of history, he regarded capitalism as a flawed and transient phase of economic progress.

Marx saw all of human history as the story of a succession of dominant economic systems. For instance, he argued, European feudalism had given way to mercantilism, which itself had been replaced by capitalism. Capitalism, he believed, would itself be overthrown on the path to communism.

According to Marx, capitalism is underpinned by a social division between the minority who own the means of production (the bourgeoisie) and the mass of wage-laborers (the proletariat), whom he considered to be exploited by the bourgeoisie. This exploitation, he argued, would result in a conflict in which the masses overthrew their economic masters. As he wrote in *The Communist Manifesto* of 1848: "The history of all hitherto existing society is the history of class struggles."

workers of the world unite

To explain how the proletariat are exploited under capitalism, Marx developed a labor theory of value. In order to turn a profit, in his view, the bourgeoisie establish the price of any given good or service by adding the cost of wages to the cost of raw materials, then adding a profit margin. The worker necessarily adds value for which he is not rewarded (the profit), while the business owner has an interest in keeping wages low (an easily achieved goal where an expanding population ensures labor is plentiful). Furthermore, owners, greedy for personal enrichment, introduce technological innovations that both reduce the need for workers and demand labor specialization, trapping employees into unsatisfying jobs and breeding self-alienation.

Marx also believed that the competitive nature of capitalism leads to a natural drift toward monopolies, concentrating wealth in the hands of an ever-smaller group. And, since the profit motive tends toward overproduction as producers seek to satisfy demand (allied to a reduction in demand as the spending capacity of the proletariat is strangled by low wages), capitalism breeds regular economic crises. Amid this turmoil, Marx believed, the proletariat (swelled by increasing numbers of disgruntled unemployed as well as members of the bourgeoisie fallen on hard times) will rise up and overthrow the capitalist system in what Marx considered to be the inexorable "march of history." Capitalism would be replaced by a type of socialism in which the proletariat wrestled control of economic resources, which, in turn, would evolve into communism where there is no private property and everything is commonly owned. Marx famously urged:

Let the ruling classes tremble at a Communistic revolution. The proletarians have nothing to lose but their chains. They have a world to win. Working men of all countries, unite!

Of course, his doctrine had an enormous effect on 20th-century history, as communism was widely adopted, most notably by Russia and China. While the collapse of the Soviet Union and the Eastern Bloc, along with the economic liberalization of China, seem to have signaled the death knell for Marxist ideology, the economic turmoil of recent years has nonetheless brought renewed interest to his teachings.

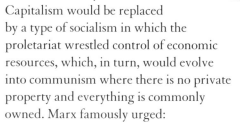

Karl Marx

Karl Marx was born in 1818 in Prussia (now part of Germany). He studied law and philosophy, becoming a devotee of the philosopher Hegel. Marx edited a newspaper in Cologne before moving to Paris in the early 1840s. Disillusioned with life under the capitalist system, he adopted an increasingly radical socialist outlook. In Paris he met Friedrich Engels, with whom he would write some of his most important work. After being expelled from France, Marx spent time in Belgium before moving to London. In 1848, he and Engels wrote *The Communist Manifesto*. That same year a wave of radical revolutions were snuffed out across Europe, to Marx's disappointment. He briefly went back to Germany before returning to London, where he spent the rest of his life, writing and speaking extensively and relying heavily on Engels for financial support.

Marx published the first volume of his most influential work, *Capital: A Critique of Political Economy* (*Das Kapital*) in 1858. He died, destitute, in 1883. The second and third volumes of *Das Kapital* appeared posthumously in 1885 and 1894, and Russia became the world's first communist state in 1917. While his political ideology is largely discredited today, much of Marx's economic analysis—for instance, his exploration of the complex relationship between labor and economic development, capital accumulation, and the nature of the business cycle—has enduring value.

less for more

When a business looks at how much to produce to maximize profits, it must consider the impact of what economists term diminishing returns–a factor that may persuade a business to stop increasing production.

Any business has two types of costs:

- **Fixed costs—costs that remain the same no matter how much the business is producing. For instance, rent on office space or the cost of machinery.**
- **Variable costs—costs that change depending on how much is being produced. These may include wages and the cost of raw materials.**

Let's return to our artisan bakery. The owner buys an oven for $2000. This is a fixed cost. If the bakery bakes 1000 loaves, the average fixed cost per loaf is $2 ($2000 divided by 1000). If it bakes 2000 loaves, the average fixed cost drops to $1 ($2000 divided by 2000). Average fixed costs continually drop as production increases.

However, the same cannot be said for variable costs. Imagine the bakery pays an employee $500 per week. If they produce 1000 loaves, the average variable cost is $500 divided by 1000, or 50 cents per loaf. However, the single employee is stretched to breaking point, so the bakery employs a second worker to share the tasks. As a result of improved efficiency, the two produce 2200 loaves. Now the average variable cost of each loaf is $1000 (the cost of their combined wages) divided by 2200, or about 45 cents per loaf. This is an example of increasing returns, since the amount of return increases as a new input is added. Worker 1's marginal output is 1000 loaves, but Worker 2's marginal output is 1200. All good so far....

too many cooks
Now the bakery employs a third worker, but their presence has less of an impact. Production increases, but only to 3250 loaves per week. The average marginal cost is thus $1500 (the cost of the combined wages) divided by 3250, or just over 46 cents per loaf. The situation in which additional outputs bring smaller increases in returns is known as "diminishing returns." If everything else remains the same in the bakery (for instance, the boss doesn't buy a second bread oven), each subsequent new employee(s) will bring diminishing returns.

Now, to work out the average total cost of each loaf, you need to add the average fixed cost and average variable cost and divide the sum by the number of loaves produced. The final figure required to work out the optimum level of production is the marginal cost—in other words, the cost of producing an additional unit (a loaf). This is calculated by dividing the change in total cost by the change in quantity of units. While the marginal cost lags behind the marginal revenue—the additional revenue brought in by each additional unit—it is worthwhile for a company to keep producing at that level. But as soon as the marginal cost is greater than the marginal revenue, it makes sense to hold back production.

to bake or not to bake?

The table shows the various total, average, and marginal costs for our bakery. Say that the bakery sells its loaves for 95 cents each. The optimum level of production is at a point where both average total costs and marginal costs are below that figure. By looking at the data, we can see that this is at a point somewhere between 6,000 and 6,500 loaves a week under the current business model.

Employee(s)	Output (loaves)	Fixed costs	Average fixed costs	Variable costs	Average variable costs	Total costs	Average total costs	Marginal costs
0	0	2000	-	0	-	2000	-	-
1	1000	2000	2.00	500	0.50	2500	2.50	0.33
2	2200	2000	0.91	1000	0.45	3000	1.36	0.41
3	3250	2000	0.62	1500	0.46	3500	1.10	0.48
4	4250	2000	0.47	2000	0.47	4000	0.94	0.50
5	5150	2000	0.39	2500	0.49	4500	0.87	0.56
6	6000	2000	0.33	3000	0.50	5000	0.83	0.58
7	6500	2000	0.31	3500	0.54	5500	0.85	1.00
8	6800	2000	0.29	4000	0.59	6000	0.88	1.67
9	6950	2000	0.29	4500	0.65	6500	0.94	3.33

big is better

While small businesses can always find ways to prosper, private enterprise is increasingly populated by big beasts with the muscle to cast aside their rivals. So what gives a large company the advantage over a smaller one?

Since the Industrial Revolution saw small-scale cottage industries give way to large factories, virtually every economic sector is now dominated by huge, multinational businesses. This is chiefly because their size allows them to take advantage of economies of scale, a term that refers to cost advantages that enable large organizations to produce a good or service more cheaply than smaller ones. A large company is more likely, for instance, to have a large workforce, allowing individual workers to become specialized in particular tasks and thus more efficient. Furthermore, a big firm is more likely to be able to use machinery and other fixed capital to its maximum capacity.

bringing home the bread

As we saw in the previous section, increased production reduces the fixed costs of each unit. Imagine that our artisan bakery discovers a big bread factory is opening just up the road. While the artisan bakery has only enough physical space to produce 6000 loaves per week from its one oven, the factory has three similar ovens plus the staff and space to produce 36,000 loaves per week (12,000 per oven). Therefore, the average fixed cost of the loaves made in the factory is exactly half that of those baked in the artisan bakery. The factory may also be able to negotiate a better price when buying equipment and machinery because they are purchasing in bigger volumes. In addition, the factory can continue to function even if one of its ovens goes wrong or a member of staff is taken ill, whereas the artisan bakery will struggle under similar circumstances.

Larger companies are also better able to absorb risk. If the factory boss believes that there is more potential profit in selling croissants than bread, she may reallocate resources so as to produce, say, 3000 croissants as an experiment one week. Correspondingly, she reduces bread production by 3000 loaves (or 12.5%) safe in the knowledge that the business can shoulder the potential loss even if she sells none of her croissants. The artisan baker, by contrast, would have to halve his bread production in order to test the croissant market in a similar fashion, leaving him at far greater commercial risk.

how did Henry Ford use economies of scale?

There is perhaps no figure in history who better manipulated economies of scale than U.S. industrialist Henry Ford. Although he was not an immediate success—he was once forced to file for bankruptcy, and it was only with his third company that he hit upon a winning formula—Ford embraced technological innovation and new labor practices to build a company that came to dominate the motor industry completely. His stroke of genius was to perfect the moving assembly line. He built specialist factories that allowed cars to be put together in an ultra-efficient way by workers who each carried out a single aspect of the manufacturing process. He offset the risk of losing staff bored by the monotonous nature of their work by paying them above the industry standard. He further reduced costs by keeping his designs simple and unadorned, convinced that the market did not want the "bells and whistles" that high-end rivals such as Rolls-Royce offered.

Ford's greatest triumph was the Model T, the first motorcar designed for mass ownership, of which 15 million vehicles had been sold before its withdrawal in 1927. By manipulating economies of scale, he took an object that had once been for the rich only and made it accessible to ordinary people. In doing so, he created an industrial model replicated around the world in the decades since.

could you repeat the question?

In 1979, Daniel Kahneman and Amos Tversky published one of the most important papers in the history of behavioral economics. Entitled "Prospect Theory: An Analysis of Decisions Under Risk," it analyzed how an individual may reach an entirely different decision depending on how a question is framed. That a person may reach different conclusions as a result of a little rephrasing suggested that the notion of the rational consumer was seriously flawed. In particular, their paper highlighted how the classical view of consumers as risk-averse, risk-seeking, or risk-neutral was oversimplified and erroneous. Instead, using empirical evidence to back their hypothesis, they showed that people are risk-loving if faced with the prospect of a loss but risk-averse if offered the prospect of a gain. To put it another way, people are more loss-averse than gain-loving. For example, if an individual is offered a guaranteed $100 or the 50% chance of being given $300, Kahneman and Tversky found most people would opt for the safe $100. However, when the question was reversed so that subjects were offered the choice of an inevitable $100 loss or else a 50% chance of a $300 loss, most of those who previously accepted the risk-averse $100 gain now went for the risk-seeking option—the 50/50 chance of a $300 loss. Fear of any loss at all caused them to chance their arm, despite the fact that the odds of success and failure in both propositions were identical.

Big is not always beautiful, though. Small companies often have the ability to respond to changing market conditions. For example, the artisan bakery might choose to produce a few dozen croissants overnight if that's what the market demands, whereas a factory boss may have to wait weeks or months for approval by senior management. Furthermore, it is often easier to marshal and motivate a smaller workforce. Large firms must therefore set the advantages of economies of scale against the disadvantages of running a bigger organization.

the (ir)rational consumer

From Adam Smith onward, most economists have assumed the existence of Economic Man (Latin name: *Homo economicus*)—a rational being who makes economic decisions after a full evaluation of all the relevant facts.

The argument goes that we make our economic decisions with a view to maximizing our happiness and well-being for the least cost and effort on our part. This self-interest ensures we undertake a sensible analysis of all the options available to us. Will I get more pleasure from an exotic holiday or by using the money to build a conservatory? Will that new sports car give me enough satisfaction to outweigh the grief my partner will give me for not spending the money on them? We are constantly making such cost–benefit analyses and so, as Smith and his disciples had it, we may be considered as rational consumers.

However, there is an increasingly large body of economists who feel that our rationality is overemphasized and even that often our decision-making is rooted in irrationality. Those who believe that we put too much weight on our status as rational beings point, for instance, to the fact that the world is so complex and interrelated that we cannot possibly work out all the costs and benefits of every decision we make. As U.S. economist Herbert Simon concluded in the 1950s, our rationality is bounded. Instead we rely on a mixture of instinct, habit, past experience, social mores, and broad rules of thumb.

method or madness?

Furthermore, rationality is extremely fluid. What might be rational for one person is certainly not for the next. For example, it is not rational for most of us to drive our cars at 200 mph (in fact, it is patently irrational) but for a highly skilled motor-racing driver being paid millions to do just that, it is eminently reasonable. Furthermore, some of our choices may be rational in the short term but irrational in the long term. Consider the person on a night out who decides to buy one last bottle of wine before heading home. At the moment they purchase the drink, they rationalize that it will provide a perfect end to a wonderful evening. However, that decision looks less rational if they wake up with a hangover the next morning, resulting in them making a mistake at work that costs them their job. Nor is it logical if, for instance, their love of wine ultimately results in serious health issues.

A growing realization that decision-making is subject to psychological, social, intellectual, and emotional factors beyond rationality has led to the rise of a whole new branch of economics, known as behavioral economics. While our irrationality had been acknowledged for several decades beforehand, behavioral economics came to prominence in the 1970s through the work of such figures as Herbert Simon, Amos Tversky, and Daniel Kahneman.

game theory

In the 1940s economists began to look seriously at game theory, which investigates decision-making in strategic situations where the actions of one agent affect the benefits or losses received by another.

In 1944, two U.S. mathematicians, Oskar Morgenstern and John von Neumann, published *Theory of Games and Economic Behavior*, which explored how economic behavior can be skewed by the activities of a few players—for instance, governments or firms with dominant market share. They looked at a series of theoretical zero-sum games (in which, typically, there are two participants, with one winner and one loser emerging) in the hope of establishing some ground

rules as to how we strategize when considering the actions of others in our decision-making processes.

While Morgenstern and von Neumann looked at games where participants could confer in order to take the most beneficial course of action, John Nash took game theory on a stage further in the 1950s by looking at what happens when agents make decisions independent of each other (as is often the case in real-life economic situations). His major breakthrough was to establish the existence of what has become known as the Nash equilibrium. This is defined as the situation in which no agent has an incentive to reconsider their course of action given the strategies chosen by the other agents. It is possible for a game to have zero or multiple Nash equilibriums.

the prisoner's dilemma

The most famous game-theory scenario is known as the prisoner's dilemma, devised by two other U.S. mathematicians, Merrill Flood and Melvin Dresher. The basic version of the game sees two criminals under arrest and unable to communicate with each other. Each is presented with the choice to testify against their associate or not. They are told that if they both testify against each other, they will get a mid-level sentence (say, four years) but if both stay silent, each will receive a shorter sentence (one year perhaps). However, if one testifies and the other doesn't, the one who testifies will be set free and the other will receive a long sentence (ten years). Since the two can't act together, logic suggests that the self-interest of each prisoner is best served by choosing to betray. This is because by doing so each prisoner gets a preferential pay-off regardless of what the other one does. For instance, if Prisoner A betrays but Prisoner B stays silent, Prisoner A is set free. But if B also betrays, A still serves a shorter sentence than if he'd stayed silent. If both stayed silent, they would serve the shortest cumulative sentence, but that does not make it the best strategy for the two information-deprived individuals.

Game theory has implications that extend into all areas of life. It is a fast-evolving field of study, with today's game theorists wrestling with questions such as the effect that repetition of a game has on subsequent decision-making, and how negative-sum games (in which the game itself can deplete the resources to be allocated) play out differently to zero-sum games.

John Nash

John Nash was born in 1928 in Bluefield, West Virginia. From a early age it was clear that he was prodigiously talented in mathematics, and in 1948 he won a scholarship to Princeton. In works including *Equilibrium Points in N-person Games* and *The Bargaining Problem* (both 1950) he developed his ideas on game theory, culminating in the formulation of the Nash equilibrium. He also carried out ground-breaking studies into algebraic geometry. In 1951, he was appointed to the staff of the Massachusetts Institute of Technology (MIT). He also worked for RAND Corporation, a thinktank that undertook research for the U.S. armed services. In 1957, he married Alicia Larde. Two years on, he was diagnosed with paranoid schizophrenia, a condition he would battle for decades. He and Alicia divorced in 1961 but remarried 40 years later.

In the 1960s and 1970s Nash continued to hold academic posts, including at Princeton, but his mental-health problems meant he was increasingly marginalized. Nonetheless, he continued to take on some of the toughest questions in mathematics. From the 1980s his health began to improve, and in 1994 he received the Nobel Prize for Economics for his work on game theory. He came to wider attention when, in 2001, his life story was turned into an Oscar-winning movie, *A Beautiful Mind*, based on the 1998 biography by Sylvia Nasar. He and his wife were killed in a car accident in New Jersey in 2015.

getting down to business

Any enterprise engaged in industrial, professional or commercial activity—whether for-profit or not-for-profit—qualifies as a business. But businesses come in many shapes and sizes.

Traditionally, businesses operate in one of three main sectors (although some are so large their activities span more than one):

- **The primary sector, which deals with natural resources and raw materials. This tends to be the dominant sector in developing economies.**
- **The secondary sector, processing raw materials into finished products.**
- **The tertiary sector, offering services ranging from banking and IT support to cleaning and catering. Service sectors are most dominant in developed economies.**

Commercial activities can, of course, be conducted by individuals working alone and who are legally indistinct from their business—such enterprises are known as sole traders—but most business is done by companies. Companies are better suited to conducting large-scale and complex business activities. "Company" derives from the Old French word *compaignie*, referring to a group of soldiers. A company, then, is like an army going into commercial battle.

One of the defining characteristics of a company is that it has a legal foundation distinct from the individuals working within it. In technical terms, it is a legal personality comprised of a group of individuals. A company can own property, sign contracts, owe tax, employ people, sue other legal entities (and be sued), irrespective of changes to the personnel who own it or work within it. That is to say, a company lives independently of the people connected to it, which gives added security to all those operating within it or dealing with it as a third party. A company only dies when it is legally wound up.

in good company

Companies are state-owned, privately owned, or publicly held:

- **A state-owned company is one owned and run by the government of a country. Examples might include a railway company, such as France's SNCF.**

how does the internet reduce friction?

Classical economics assumes that buyers and sellers within a market will find each other and have full information about all the other options in the market so that a correct price can be established. However, a little common sense tells us that this is not the case in reality. Consider, for example, how long it can take to match someone looking to buy a house with someone selling a suitable property. There are what economists refer to as search frictions as buyers and sellers aim to find each other. These frictions include time lost in searching, inconvenience, and financial penalties (for instance, paying rent while househunting). But the rise in recent years of the internet and e-commerce—the buying and selling of goods and services over the internet—has gone some way to reducing these search frictions. There is, perhaps, no clearer example of this than eBay, the open-access auction site. Established in 1995, the site's core business allows registered users to put up for sale virtually anything (bar a very few exceptions)—from superyachts to paperclips, stuffed animals to art works—even corn flakes nibbled by the rich and famous. Operating in cyberspace outside of time or geographical restrictions, if an object has a market it will find a buyer somewhere in the world, and the auction function ensures it sells for an optimum price.

going public

Companies tend to "go public" when they reach a significant size and need an influx of investment to move to the next level. By publicly floating their stock, companies can secure huge new cash streams—$16 billion flooded into Facebook when it went public in 2012. However, going public is not something to be entered into lightly. The original owners reduce their overall holding in the company by inviting in new co-owners. All shareholders have a right to vote on major company decisions, which can make the decision-making process far more complicated. Furthermore, public companies are open to much greater scrutiny from regulators and must publish their accounts. Nonetheless, the vast majority of the world's biggest companies are publicly owned.

- A privately owned company is owned by an individual or two or more partners who retain full responsibility for any debt incurred by the business. Private companies do not have to release details of their accounts to the public. Most companies start out privately owned, and some of the world's biggest firms decide to stay that way. For example, the investment bank Goldman Sachs has remained in private hands.
- A public company is one that has offered its securities (its stocks, shares, and bonds, for example) to the general public. These securities may then be traded to other members of the public, classically on stock exchanges. Shareholders also receive a dividend—a share of the company's profits in proportion to the number of shares owned.

cornering the market

For markets to work, it is generally considered essential that there is genuine competition between suppliers. Nonetheless, sometimes the market for a particular good or service is dominated by a single company.

When one company controls all of a market it is known as a monopoly. When control is shared by only a small group of companies, we refer to it as an oligopoly. Often monopolies and oligopolies are regarded with suspicion by consumers and authorities alike, since the inherent absence of competition means that companies have greater capacity to ignore the demands of consumers. There is the absence of incentive to provide goods and services of the highest quality, to innovate, to provide customer care, or to keep prices down. In fact, a company with a monopoly knows that consumers who want what they are selling have no choice but to pay whatever price is demanded or else simply do without.

To avoid such situations, most countries operate antimonopolistic (also known as antitrust) legislation. Many states have government agencies whose sole purpose is to assess the business practices of companies and the impact of mergers and takeovers to ensure a monopoly is not created. Among the most high-profile subjects of antitrust investigations in recent years has been the computing giant, Microsoft, whose Windows operating system and Internet Explorer web browser came to dominate the international market, prompting accusations that competition was stifled.

the land of big giants

While monopolies are generally considered bad for the consumer, the reverse is true for the business that achieves a monopoly. For instance, a monopolist (a business that has a monopoly) can expect increased profits, can benefit from economies of scale, and theoretically have greater resources to invest in research and development. That is why large companies always aim to secure the maximum market share possible within legal limits. At the beginning of the 20th century John D. Rockefeller argued that his oil monopoly brought order to a sector where unrestrained competition had previously brought chaos. (Although, significantly, Rockefeller's business practices were pivotal to the evolution of antitrust law in the U.S.) A century or so later, Bill Gates defended Microsoft's market dominance by arguing that the company was not monopolistic but that its products were so good that everybody wanted them.

It is true, too, that governments can facilitate monopolies by granting patents on new inventions. A patent can produce an effective monopoly for the duration of the patent, but authorities may deem this justifiable, since without guaranteed commercial returns businesses may feel it is not in their interests to invest in research and development. For example, a drug company may only be willing to spend billions to develop a treatment for AIDS if it knows it will be able to recoup the investment by securing eventual market dominance for a fixed period of time. Thus, monopolies are generally regarded as bad for the consumer but with exceptions.

what is a natural monopoly?

A natural monopoly occurs when the cost of entering a market is so high that only a single company can realistically make a profit. The most usual reason that a natural monopoly occurs is that the industry in question demands a vast initial outlay on technological equipment. For example, the cost of establishing a grid to supply a city with electricity is such that it only makes sense for a single company to make that investment. In other words, the capital cost of joining the market for anything less than a market-dominant share of the business is a huge disincentive to potential competitors. Conversely, a natural monopolist is able to exploit economies of scale necessary for the efficient running of the sector. Utilities industries—such as electricity, gas, and water—are often characterized by natural monopolies. Other examples might include railways, road networks, and even space agencies.

As with any other monopoly, there is potential for the supplier to abuse its position of power at the consumer's expense, so governments often step in to regulate natural monopolies—many countries have, for instance, created state agencies to oversee their water and power industries to ensure that supply is kept up, standards are maintained, and prices pegged at a reasonable level for consumers.

keeping order

Evidence of serious mismanagement in the financial sector, allied to scandals such as that which overtook Enron early in this century, has seen corporate governance come under the spotlight.

Corporate governance describes all the rules, regulations, policies, and processes that a business follows to ensure that everything it does is above board. When it works, corporate governance aims to protect the interests of all the stakeholders in a company—including the owners, management, customers, business partners, suppliers, and society at large. Corporate governance therefore covers everything from how the company conducts its business and what level of commercial risk it is prepared to shoulder, to how employees treat each other in the workplace and how the business meets its environmental responsibilities.

But in whose interest is a business really run? The customer? Wider society? It's a nice idea, but is rarely the case when it comes to profit-making firms. It is generally accepted (and often legally mandated) in free-market environments that companies are run primarily in the interests of their owners (whether an individual, a family, or an army of shareholders). In other words, it is to the owners that a firm's management is answerable. However, in the 1930s, U.S. economists Adolf Berle and Gardiner Means argued that, in fact, the greatest power often lies in the hands of management—particularly when a large number of shareholders struggle to exert a unified presence or where shareholders have only a short-term interest in the company's health (hedge-fund investors, for example).

too powerful for their own good

There is nothing inherently wrong with management wielding great power. However, should owner and management interests diverge, there is clearly a problem. Berle and Means' answer, and one which became enshrined in law, was to give shareholders and company owners greater powers to hire and fire. Fast-forward to the present day, and we have a situation where taxpayers have a hand in some of the world's biggest businesses as a result of the global upheaval of recent years. Not unreasonably, they want to know why their money has been diverted toward saving numerous megarich, blue-chip companies.

Of course, there is no single answer, but the emergence of an overmighty layer of management in many companies seems to bear at least partial responsibility. Driven by a desire for self-enrichment, there is evidence that some managers took crucial business decisions not in shareholders' interests (let alone third-party interests) but to unsure that short-term profit targets were met in order to trigger bonus payments. According to this theory, some bankers were drawn to ultra-high-risk investments that offered short-term paper profits rather than assessing the real long-term prospects of these investments.

While the Great Recession of the late 2000s that hit economies across the planet prompted a debate on how best to improve corporate governance, it is not yet clear whether there is the political will to push through reform. For a generation of financiers and politicians brought up on a credo of deregulation, it would be a bitter pill to swallow. But if public confidence in the commercial world is to be restored, there may be no choice.

what does the boss get paid?

One of the great bones of contention in recent times has been executive pay. Since the 1980s, there has been a trend toward increasing remuneration for senior executives at a level that far outstrips the general rise in earnings. For instance, in the U.S., in 2013, the CEO-to-worker pay ratio was 273:1. In the mid-1960s it was 20:1. To rub salt into the wound, CEOs of the U.S.'s top 350 publicly traded companies saw their earnings rise by 37% between 2009 and 2012, as the rest of the economy struggled to rouse itself from the doldrums. Those who defend high executive pay use a simple argument: you get what you pay for. A good CEO doubtless adds massive value to a company. One need only look at Steve Jobs at Apple to see how the right man at the helm can positively impact a business.

However, the pitch is somewhat queered because those who agree executive pay (commonly, the company's directors) often have a vested interest in keeping rates high, since they are likely to be beneficiaries of generous remuneration packages themselves. Furthermore, as evidenced by the global financial crisis, high pay does not necessarily correspond to good management. When things go badly wrong and a CEO is forced from office, they often leave with a hefty golden handshake (a contractually agreed pay-off). Many observers see this as the opposite of capitalist ideology as failure reaps the outgoing boss significant rewards.

knowledge is power

The classical economic model takes for granted that all those participating in a market have equal access to the necessary information to make informed choices. In practice this may not happen.

In a competitive market economy, in theory a consumer needs to know only a few basics to strike a deal: what they want; which products are available that fit the bill; what each product's specifications are; and how much they are being sold for. But in reality, different players in a market are often in possession of wildly varying amounts of relevant information. For instance, a house seller aware of antisocial neighbors or of imminent building works may keep such details from a potential buyer for fear of losing the sale or perhaps having to agree to a lower price. Alternatively, imagine a buyer who works at the town hall and who has heard whispers that the local authorities are about to fund a regeneration of the city center. They may choose to keep this intelligence to themselves, buying the house at current prices in the expectation of selling it on for much more after the regeneration.

too little knowledge can be a dangerous thing

The party with superior information is always well placed to strike a deal tipped in their favor. However, such deals are not good for the economy as a whole. One famous example was provided in U.S. economist George Akerloff's 1970 paper "The Market for Lemons." He examined the used-car market—one in which sellers usually have far more knowledge of the product than buyers. This "asymmetric information," he argued, creates buyer uncertainty, so that buyers become unwilling to pay too high a price. As a result, those sellers with high-quality cars for sale become reluctant to put them on the market, so that the market becomes distorted toward lower-quality cars. In other words, the imbalance in information leads to a failure of the market.

Clearly, it pays to be well informed, a fact traders grasped long ago. The earliest exchanges, such as the medieval Ter Beurse in Bruges, were often connected to hostelries because these were places where travelers convened and shared information. Reports of crop failure or imminent war in a far-off land could have serious repercussions for the local price of grain or bronze.

can you know too much?

Such is the proliferation of information available today that some analysts have argued that it actually skews the markets. For example, there is evidence to suggest that a market downturn can be accelerated if it receives intense media scrutiny while it is playing out. The news, as it were, drives the decline. Furthermore, the automatic, super-speedy processing of raw data by advanced algorithmic programs has seen markets go into spins without rhyme or reason. These programs—modeled by mathematicians so as to predict market movements on the basis of statistical analysis—have made possible High Frequency Trades, in which holdings are traded and moved on again within the space of a few seconds with no recourse to human intervention.

That's all well and good when the system works, but technical failures can lead to disaster—such as the notorious 2010 U.S. Flash Crash, when some half a billion dollars was lost by investors in a day thanks to a technical hitch. Then there is the problem of insider dealing, whereby traders unfairly gain access to non-public information (such as profit forecasts or plans for a merger) and illegally use that knowledge to manipulate the markets. While the penalties for such behavior can be severe, the potential rewards continue to tempt traders to veer from the path of righteousness all too often. So you can be too well informed after all.

competitive edge

Traders have always exploited the best available technology to get the latest news first, giving them the competitive edge—from using the speediest horsemen and employing carrier pigeons to the modern era of rolling news services and specialist data services (such as the industry-standard, electronic Bloomberg Platform). It is widely believed that banking magnate Nathan Rothschild had such an efficient communications network that he knew the result of the Battle of Waterloo a full day before the British king!

-4.85% 0.01

-13.04% 0.00

-50.00% 0.0

Pareto efficiency

Pareto efficiency is a theory devised by the Franco-Italian economist, Vilfredo Pareto, and describes the efficient allocation of economic resources. It has widespread applications, from determining production efficiency to guiding welfare policy.

Pareto efficiency is said to be achieved when it is impossible to raise the welfare of one party without lowering the welfare of another. By extension, a Pareto improvement can be described as the situation where you can make one agent better off without making another worse off.

In terms of production efficiency, for instance, a Production Possibility Frontier

or PPF (see page 117) is considered as Pareto-efficient, since the frontier represents the limit at which production of one product cannot be increased without reducing the production of another. However, any point to the left of the PPF is considered Pareto-inefficient, since production can be increased on one product without necessarily impacting the production of the other.

efficiency and fairness

In terms of resource-allocation efficiency, Pareto efficiency demands that no one can be made better off without negatively impacting the well-being of someone else. That, though, does not mean that resources need necessarily be distributed fairly. Imagine that you have two pints of coffee and two pints of tea. You give Jack two pints of coffee and a pint of tea, while Jill gets the other pint of tea. This is not, by common understanding, equitable distribution, but it is nonetheless Pareto-efficient since no one is worse off than they were before you distributed the drink.

Of course, in real life there are lots of goods and services, and people have differing tastes, so let's consider Jack and Jill in a slightly different scenario. If Jack has all the coffee and tea, that is an inefficient distribution of resources. Now, imagine that Jack loves coffee and hates tea, while Jill loves tea but hates coffee. In this case, if some of the coffee is taken from Jack and given to Jill, there is a Pareto improvement, since Jill benefits and Jack loses nothing. However, if both like coffee and tea, they can swap a proportion of their tea and coffee until the optimal allocation has been achieved. By trading in this way, the two can reach a compromise where they both feel the benefit of the addition of the other's drink without feeling the loss of their own.

Echoing Adam Smith's "invisible hand" (see page 17), it was Pareto's belief that the welfare of society is thus best served when individuals trade in their own self-interest until they reach Pareto efficiency. This, he believed, was preferable to relying on governments to make value judgments as to how best to meet the needs of their people—in our example by giving everyone a fixed volume of tea when some people would rather have coffee. However, critics of Pareto and his theory point out that, as we saw with Jack and Jill initially, a society might achieve Pareto efficiency and still be riven by inequality.

Vilfredo Pareto

Vilfredo Pareto was born in Paris in 1848, the son of an Italian noble and his French wife. The family returned to Italy when Pareto was a young boy. He graduated with a doctorate in engineering from Turin and embarked on a career as a civil engineer. Boasting liberal political leanings, by the mid-1880s he had changed career path, lecturing in economics at the University of Florence. He married in 1889, but the union ended in divorce in 1902. From 1893 until his death, he resided in Switzerland, having been appointed chair of political economy at the University of Lausanne. He became a leading figure in the so-called Lausanne School of economics, whose members made significant contributions to the development of microeconomics.

As well as defining Pareto efficiency, Pareto also proposed the Pareto principle (based on his observation that 80% of Italy's land was owned by 20% of the population; the principle, which adherents say has wide-ranging applications, states that 80% of effects are achieved by 20% of causes) and Pareto distribution (an equation that he held explains historically recurring patterns of wealth distribution). Much of the work of his later years was concerned with sociology. He was married for a second time, to Jeanne Regis, shortly before his death in 1923 in Geneva. His major publications include *Course of Political Economy* (1897), *Socialist Systems* (1902), *Manual of Political Economy* (1906), and *Mathematical Economics* (1911).

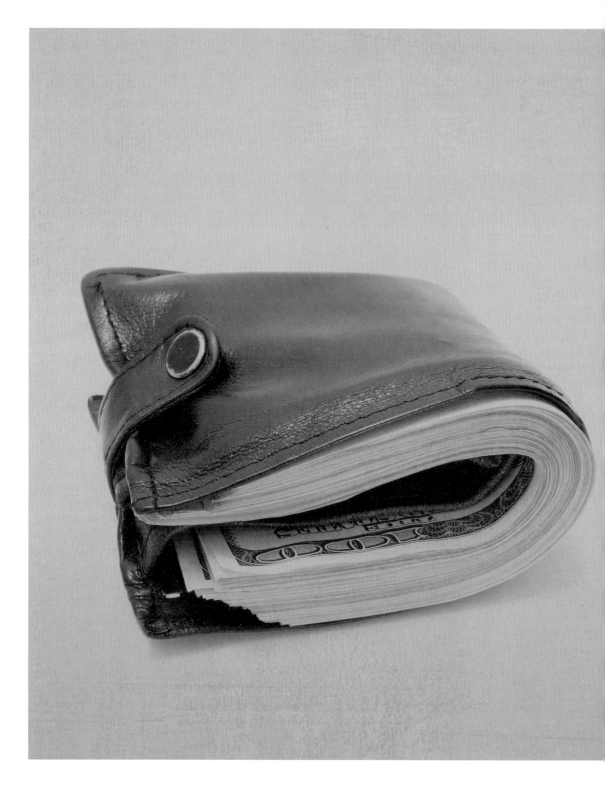

how do personal finances work?

banking on it

waiting for a rainy day

buy now, pay later

speculate to accumulate

small is beautiful

silver linings

pass it on

bankruptcy

giving it away

economics is everywhere

or a dividend), borrowers pay for their loan (through interest payments or some other kind of security), while the bank takes a cut for acting as intermediary.

horses for courses

For most of us, the first financial institution we become familiar with is the bank, an institution licensed to receive deposits and make loans. Here are some examples of the main types:

banking on it

For better and worse, we rely on the financial-services sector. Since the birth of modern banking in 15th-century Renaissance Italy, the sector has been opaque and often distrusted. So what do the banks do for us?

The financial sector is made up of many different types of institution, including banks, insurance companies (which accept premiums in return for offsetting the potential cost of specific risks), mortgage lenders (which provide loans for real-estate purchases), and investment funds (such as hedge funds, which take speculative positions in markets in the hope of high returns). The sector comprises a vast array of business models—from very high to very low risk—but in the end they all do much the same thing: they connect those in possession of money with those who need it. Investors receive a return on their money (for instance, in the form of interest

- **Central banks—banks that typically issue currency, control a nation's money supply, and act as the "bank's bank," providing loans and overseeing regulation. (See page 120 for more.)**
- **Supranational banks—banks that operate across two or more countries, with the aim of bolstering the economic development of its members. Examples include the World Bank, the European Central Bank, and the European Bank for Reconstruction and Development. (See Big Beasts on page 162).**
- **Commercial banks—also known as retail banks. These deal with the general public, accepting deposits and granting loans to businesses and individuals. Additional services might include mortgage-broking and currency exchange.**
- **Investment banks—also known as merchant banks. Investment banks (and investment divisions of commercial banks) usually deal with companies**

rather than members of the public. They aim to help firms access capital by, for instance, underwriting loans, assisting with share issues, and advising on mergers and acquisitions.

- Private banks—institutions that specialize in managing the wealth of the rich (sometimes referred to as high-net-worth individuals or HNWIs).

Banks look to maximize their profits by exploiting economies of scale. Having accrued a body of deposits, a bank retains sufficient cash to cover customer withdrawals and puts the remainder into a range of investments (some low-risk and low-return, others higher-risk and higher-return). The bigger the bank, the lower its average costs, so the more it can spread risk and the greater its potential profits.

However, as we have seen in recent years, even the biggest banks can fall victim to overly risky investments, as well as to runs on a bank, when customers demand the return of their deposits in unexpectedly high numbers.

how do phones help the world's "unbanked"?

While it is often hard to love the financial sector, we might want to bear in mind that life without banks can be tough. An estimated half of the world's population currently have no bank account, with that figure rising to three-quarters in the world's poorest regions. If being unbanked sounds like a liberating notion, the truth is often quite different. It means that you have no regulated institution to look after any savings you might have. If you find yourself without the money you need at any given moment, there is no convenient ATM on hand. There is no hope of credit to help you cover the costs arising from an emergency situation, nor of a loan to start a business, nor of a mortgage to buy a property. Many unbanked people may be unable to access healthcare when they or their families most need it.

However, there is a beacon of hope for the unbanked. It is thought that over a billion of the global unbanked have access to mobile phones. Thanks to developing technologies, even those without a bank account can now use their phones to make payments, receive remittances from abroad, and access financial services previously denied them. The first few tentative steps, perhaps, to breaking long-established cycles of poverty.

waiting for a rainy day

While the temptation to "spend, spend, spend" is an easy one to which to succumb, the more economically prudent take the opportunity to squirrel away any excess money they have to use later on.

Savings equate to the amount left over after an individual's expenditure is subtracted from their income over a fixed period of time. So if your income equates to $2000 per month and your spending (on essentials and luxuries) comes to $1800, you have savings of $200 for the month. However, it is, alas, all too possible to have negative savings if you rely on credit to cover an overspend on your income. In economic terms, the proportion of our disposable income that we desire to save is a measure of our propensity to save; the proportion of additional income that we want to save is a measure of our marginal propensity to save.

The great thing about savings, needless to say, is that the capital sum can be made to work for you so that it increases in value over time. You might, for example, choose to deposit it with one of the financial institutions described in the previous section so that it accrues interest. Alternatively, you might place it into a pension fund, to be accessed later in life, or make investments (see page 94). You could even decide to use your savings to start a new business. These plans of action come with differing degrees of risk, but all offer the chance to expand your savings pot by opening up new revenue streams—something you will never achieve if you hide your spare cash under the mattress.

spending to flourish

Yet, for the economist looking at the wider economy, saving is not always a good thing. In simple terms, if people are saving a larger proportion of their incomes, it means they are spending less, and an economy in which people are not spending freely is likely to stagnate. However, since the 1950s, economists such as Franco Modigliani and Milton Friedman have helped to quell these fears by establishing that there is a general trend to save when you are younger (when you have more earning capacity and an awareness that this will decline in years to come) and spend when you are older. In practice, this means that there is generally a happy balance between savers and spenders at any given time, keeping consumption reasonably constant. Nonetheless, Ben Bernanke, former chairman of the U.S. Federal Reserve, posited a controversial theory that the global slowdown of the 2000s was, in part, the result of a glut of savings in countries other than the U.S. (most notably China), prompting a subsequent slow-down in international trade.

Given that saving is easier the more money you have, it is perhaps unsurprising that the richest 20% of the world's population are more likely to save than the bottom 20% (three times more likely in the developing world and twice as likely in the developed world). More remarkably, only some 20% of global saving occurs in formal financial institutions (although the level is much higher in the developed world). In the developing world, savers are far more likely to pool their savings in local, informal savings clubs or with friends and family.

how does compound interest work?

If you put your savings into an account with a bank, the chances are it will earn you compound interest. This means that once the first interest period is up, each subsequent interest payment is made on the initial capital sum plus the interest already garnered. In the table below, see how an initial deposit of $100 grows year on year when a compound interest rate of 4% is applied.

Year	Existing balance	Interest earned	New balance
1	$100	$4	$104
2	$104	$4.16	$108.16
3	$108.16	$4.33	$112.49
4	$112.49	$4.50	$116.99
5	$116.99	$4.68	$121.67
6	$121.67	$4.87	$126.54
7	$126.54	$5.06	$131.60
8	$131.60	$5.26	$136.86
9	$136.86	$5.47	$142.33
10	$143.70	$5.75	$149.45

As you can see, the capital sum has increased by just short of 50% over ten years.

buy now, pay later

While those with a bigger income than expenditure can turn their thoughts toward saving, those with spending that outpaces their income are more likely to look toward securing credit.

Credit refers to the system in which goods or services are granted to a purchaser in return for deferred, rather than immediate, payment. That is to say, the buyer agrees to pay for the good or service at a fixed point in the future. Very often, the buyer will incur an additional fee for using credit. The higher the interest rate and the longer the payment period, the more it will cost.

Modern society has come up with numerous ways of providing credit, including:

- **The bank loan**—by which a capital sum is advanced for repayment over a fixed period, normally at a fixed interest rate. Loans are either secured (giving the lender a claim on the borrower's assets in the event of a default) or unsecured (giving the lender no such claim).
- **Payday loans**, usually issued by private finance companies, are very short-term loans often available to borrowers with even poor credit ratings (a measure of a borrower's ability to successfully repay) but typically carrying punitively high interest rates.
- **The overdraft**—an agreement between a bank and customer permitting the customer to go into debit on their account up to an agreed limit and for an agreed period of time.
- **Peer-to-peer lending**—for instance, credit unions are owned and run by their members, who alone can make deposits and take out loans.
- **The installment plan**—spreading the cost of a high-value purchase over a period of months or years. Payments may or may not be interest-free. The purchaser does not own the item until the final payment has been made.
- **The credit card**—a card issued by a recognized financial institution that allows the holder to make purchases up to a preagreed limit. The retailer is instantly recompensed, with the purchaser making good the debt with the card issuer. This type of credit is known as revolving credit, since the available credit varies depending on what has been borrowed

and repaid. The holder can use the credit facility repeatedly over an extended period of time, as long as they meet minimum agreed repayments.

a credit to the system

There is an old adage that says "neither a borrower nor a lender be," but there is nothing inherently wrong with credit. Indeed, the global economy would collapse without it. Credit allows individuals and businesses to make large outlays and spread the cost over time. Imagine how many fewer big-ticket items would be sold—from televisions and fridges to cars and houses—if credit was not available. Similarly, countless businesses would never have got off the ground if their founders had needed to find the money for capital outlays out of their own pocket. Credit is vital to keeping the economy moving. Nonetheless, it has been convincingly argued that easy availability of credit (especially in the developed world) has created a culture of irresponsible spending, leaving large numbers of people with unmanageable debt burdens.

when did consumer credit begin?

Gerard Swope is one of the key figures in the consumer-credit boom, the benefits and costs of which economists continue to debate. As president of General Electric in the 1920s and 1930s, Swope sought to sell household electrical goods to the mass market and offered credit to customers as a way to drive sales. He knew there was huge demand for home electricals, such as vacuum cleaners, washing machines, and refrigerators, but, even after exploiting economies of scale, prices remained beyond the reach of many households. So he decided to allow customers to pay for their goods in monthly installments instead. He was not the first to come up with the concept, but no company as large and prestigious as General Electric had previously offered the service.

Swope's bravura was rewarded with a massive upsurge in sales. It also marked the start of a consumer boom that we are arguably still enjoying today. But, at the same time, easy credit has fueled a rapid rise in household debt. In the U.S., for instance, it rose from 15% to 32% over the 1920s and stood at a disturbingly high 127% in 2007, just as the global economic slowdown took hold. Credit has its place in the economy, but it is a beast to be controlled, not left to run wild.

speculate to accumulate

Private individuals and companies both seek to maximize their revenues over the long term by taking their capital assets (most commonly money) and using them to fund investments.

Investing is the process by which capital is directed toward an economic endeavor (say, a new business or the purchase of property) with a view to increasing income or profit in the future. In sum, an investor gives something away with the expectation of getting more back in due course.

For a business owner, it might be the purchase of a new factory or cutting-edge machinery, increased spending on wages, or training staff. In each case, the owner is investing in things that they believe will make the company more profitable in the future. Private investors, meanwhile, invest in order to boost their personal incomes.

They might decide to put money directly into a business or buy a property to rent and/or sell on. They may also decide to try their luck on the markets or, more commonly, place their money with a third party, such as an investment fund, to speculate on their behalf.

rules of engagement

Canny investors aim to manage their exposure to risk. This means developing a portfolio of high- and low-risk investments, so that the safe bets offset potential losses from the more speculative gambles.

Professional investors spend their working lives studying data and tracking trends in a bid to short-circuit risk. By way of example, in the latter decades of the 20th century it was widely believed that the risk associated with derivatives markets could be largely neutralized by spreading risk on the assumption that prices vary in a broadly predictable way. However, the disaster that befell the economic sector from 2008 was in no small part rooted in the expansion of complex financial instruments that dangerously underestimated the chance of extreme price movements. Just as we were tuning into the idea of investing as a win–win game, the rules of the game changed again.

is gold as good as it gets?

Traditionally, there have been few safer investments than gold. Over the course of history, it has maintained its value in the face of wars, crises, and disasters. It has long bewitched investors, giving it a status as a stable and reliable store of value like nothing else on earth. As a result, it has served as the cornerstone for countless currencies, with governments and central banks maintaining their national reserves in the form of gold bullion. In the aftermath of the Second World War, the global economic landscape was reconfigured by the Bretton Woods agreement (see page 162), which saw countries around the globe peg their exchange rates to the U.S. dollar, which, in turn, was pegged to the value of gold.

This system, known as the "gold standard," nonetheless had—and still has—its critics. While the gold standard is synonymous with prudence and is seen as a control on inflation, it can cause problems when a government needs to increase its spending significantly, as in a time of war. Many countries have subsequently suspended the gold standard or done away with it altogether, including the U.S. in 1971. There is now a significant school of thought that claims it is no longer fit for purpose, being unwieldy, limited in supply, and increasingly subject to price fluctuations. However, as gold continues to reach all-time price highs, it continues to win the hearts and minds of many investors.

spinning the wheel

All investments are a game of risk, in which the investor stakes their chances on a particular set of circumstances playing out. The backer of a startup company is speculating that the company will turn a profit. A speculator on the commodities markets is betting on the price of a particular commodity rising or falling at some point in the future. Other investments favor a long-term commitment. Property prices tend to rise in the long term but may fluctuate in the short-to-mid-term. Someone who pays $400,000 for a house today may find its value drops to $385,000 in six months' time but (barring disasters) will likely see a steady rise over, say, ten years.

small is beautiful

In recent decades, the boom in microfinance means opportunities for budding entrepreneurs in the developing world who would hitherto have been unable to launch their businesses.

"Microfinance" describes financial services provided to low-income groups and individuals who lack the resources to access traditional banking facilities. The sums involved tend to be low (an average microfinance loan is estimated to be about $100) but are enough to positively impact the lives of millions of people in the developing world. Microfinance has traditionally been the preserve of non-profit organizations whose principal aim is to alleviate poverty and promote sound economic management in local communities.

Typically, a microfinance provider offers three core services: loans, savings accounts, and insurance. Small loans are typically given to set up a new business, with a view to the borrower becoming financially independent in the long term. Microfinance companies provide loans to individuals and groups that traditional banks may deem too high-risk. A microfinance loan carries interest repayments but generally at a low level. Several loans may also be grouped together to spread the risk of default and in the belief that social pressures will compel borrowers to meet their liabilities if at all possible. Defaults are thought not to exceed 10% of all loans— an admirable achievement. Microfinance loans also enable borrowers to build their credit profile, raising the prospect of accessing traditional banking services in the future. Women, who are often excluded from traditional financial institutions, have been particular beneficiaries, while millions have been saved from using unscrupulous loan sharks.

Savings accounts, meanwhile, encourage economic prudence, with many borrowers obliged to save a defined portion of their income. Then there is microinsurance, characterized by low premiums and low policy values that allow the poor to pool their resources to spread risk. For example, a group of sub-Saharan farmers might join forces to insure themselves against the risk of crop blight. Many microfinance organizations also demand that applicants undertake a program of financial education and money management before being granted access to financial services.

for the common good

The modern microfinance movement took off in the 1970s. Among the innovators in the field was the Bangladeshi Grameen Bank, whose founder, Muhammad Yunus, was awarded the 2006 Nobel Peace Prize for his work. Most early microfinance bodies were either specialist banks, public-sector institutions, or non-profit non-governmental organizations, most of which expected to reinvest any profits earned into their day-to-day work. However, in more recent times—not without controversy—profit-making organizations have entered the fray.

The Compartamos Banco of Mexico, for instance, was established in 1990 on a non-profit basis but became a profit-making entity at the beginning of the millennium and was valued at $400 million when it launched on the Mexican stock exchange in 2007. Meanwhile, many established commercial banks have developed microfinance divisions, often with an eye to selling traditional financial products into new markets in the long term.

The World Bank estimates that over half a billion people have benefited directly and indirectly from the microfinance boom. It is a sector micro in scope but with the potential to make an enormous impact.

how can you stay ahead of the crowd?

The internet explosion has allowed for the blossoming of a new, innovative form of microfinance known as crowdfunding. This is a form of peer-to-peer lending, in which borrowers and lenders are matched without the need for a financial intermediary. Crowdfunding uses bespoke fundraising websites (such as Kickstarter) and social media sites in a bid to attract investors to new businesses or projects. In return for, typically, a small capital investment to help get the enterprise off the ground, lenders may expect a share of the business in a traditional investor model but may receive other non-traditional rewards—someone who invests in a crowdfunded movie could receive a producer's credit or perhaps a walk-on role in the film.

Crowdfunding can be a risky business for investors given the relatively high failure rate of startups but the model offers advantages, too. It allows entrepreneurs to access support from non-traditional sources (sources other than friends and families or risk-averse banks) and offers investors the chance to back businesses that might otherwise be closed to them. Furthermore, the crowdfunding process can itself generate invaluable publicity for a new scheme. One notably successful campaign was for the Pebble E-Paper Watch, a smart watch, which raised capital of over $10 million in 37 days in 2012.

silver linings

In an era when more of us can expect to enjoy longer lives, the pressure to plan for a financially secure future has never been greater.

On retirement, most of us will come to rely on a pension paid by the state (typically on the basis of age, but possibly other criteria, such as disability), by an employer, or by private retirement funds to their contributors. The fact that we are all living longer has heaped enormous pressure on pension providers (see page 177).

major pension types
- **A state pension is paid by a government to all qualifying individuals after a specific age (typically fixed somewhere in the range of 60–69 years) and may or may not be means-tested. The size of payment is dependent on the amount contributed by the pensioner during their working life, usually through the tax system.**

- **An occupational pension is administered by a financial institution on an employer's behalf. Such pensions can be contributory (employer and employee both make contributions during the employee's working life) or non-contributory (only the employer contributes). These pensions are typically either defined-benefit pensions (the size of regular payment relates to the employee's salary and length of service) or defined-contribution pensions (payment level is dependent on how much the employee paid in and how well the pension pot has performed in investment terms).**

- **A private or personal pension is arranged by an individual with a pension provider. The individual makes contributions into a pension scheme along with other people, and the combined pension pot is invested by the administering financial body. The size of pension depends on the investment performance of the pot. Such schemes are popular with those who do not qualify for employer pensions.**

The level of retirement pension as a percentage of working-life earnings is known as the gross pension replacement rate, and it varies markedly from country to country. The rate in Iceland, according to OECD figures in 2010, approached 97%, and in China, 78%. Germany's, meanwhile, stood at 42%—below the European Union average of 62% but above the rates in both the U.S. (39%) and the UK (32%).

will you grow old disgracefully?

The image of the young as footloose and fancy-free and the elderly as prudent and conservative is one not well supported by the evidence. According to the data-tracking company, Nielsen, for instance, almost 50% of the U.S. population will be 50 or over by 2017 and will be in possession of some 70% of total disposable income. Meanwhile, in 2012, a Japanese study found the over-60s in that country accounted for 40% of consumer spending. Euromonitor has predicted that the over-60s around the world will be responsible for $15 trillion of spending by 2020, up from $8 trillion in a decade. This is data to conjure with for a retail and advertising sector that has long focused on capturing the younger market. On the one hand, retailers must aim to meet the particular needs of the elderly (the global market in incontinence products, for example, grew by almost 50% in the five years to 2012, when it was valued at $4.7 billion); on the other, it seems those entering old age in the 21st century have a more youthful outlook than ever before. Nielsen, for instance, has found that they are responsible for purchasing some 40% of Apple Inc. products. Retailers will ignore the clout of our elders and betters at their peril.

pass it on

We are often urged to spend what we have, since "you can't take it with you." However, the last significant economic act we can make is to pass it on.

A bequest is the act of leaving money or property to an individual or organization through the provisions of a legal instrument. This is most commonly done through a will—a recognized legal document that outlines how your estate (that is, your property) is to be distributed after you die.

A will is created by the testator, and those who benefit from its terms are beneficiaries, who are usually members of the testator's family or circle of friends, but bequests may also be left to charities or other institutions, as donations or endowments (see page 104).

Someone who dies without making a will is described as intestate. To create a will you must be an adult of sound mind. The process of will-writing can be arduous and emotional, but it is, economically speaking, a very sensible thing to do. Distributing an estate when someone dies intestate can be a drawn-out and legally complicated process.

the long reach of the taxman

Writing a will ensures that your property is shared out as you wish, once your debts and liabilities have been met. It is also possible to plan to minimize the impact of estate and inheritance taxes, which are paid on inherited money or property, either on the basis of the value of the dead person's estate (estate taxes) or on the value of each beneficiary's legacy (inheritance taxes), as in many constituencies it is possible to establish a trust to administer a bequest and so reduce or even bypass tax worries. Setting up a trust is also a good method of protecting assets earmarked for someone below the age of majority or otherwise unable to manage the assets themselves.

The fairness of estate and inheritance taxes is hotly debated. For some, they are a tax on what has already been taxed. Most of us pay income tax on our earnings, so why should we pay tax on that same money when we want to pass it on? However, these taxes are also seen as a means of redistributing wealth across society. Without them, wealth passes down generations regardless of the merits (or otherwise) of the inheritors. Winston Churchill, who was born into wealth but also relied on his talents and work ethic, considered death duties to be a check against the emergence of a "race of idle rich."

what is the cost of not making your intentions clear?

When a will is disputed, it falls to the courts to decide who is entitled to what. Such cases are notoriously long and often fraught affairs—not to mention an efficient way of running down the value of an estate while filling the coffers of the lawyers involved. Among the most famous such cases is a fictional one, that of Jarndyce and Jarndyce in Charles Dickens's *Bleak House*, a suit that has come to symbolize the debilitating nature of prolonged legal disputes. There are plenty of real-life examples, too, often accompanied by the unseemly airing of one's laundry in public. One example was that of energy billionaire Fred Koch, whose four sons spent almost 20 years fighting over their inheritance, often in the public sphere, before finally ironing out their differences in 2001.

Similarly expensive and unedifying was the long-running dispute between the son of oil magnate J. Howard Marshall II and his late father's former Playboy Playmate wife, Anna Nicole Smith, which rumbled on even after Smith's death in 2007. Benjamin Franklin famously observed that nothing in this world is certain except for death and taxes. While it may be unromantic to say so, dying has economic implications to match pretty much anything we do when we are alive, so it is well worth tying up as many loose ends as possible in advance.

bankruptcy

Economics is a game of risk, profit, and loss that throws up losers as well as winners. Those who find that the game is up may decide to declare bankruptcy—a decision that opens a new chapter while closing an old one.

Bankruptcy is a legal status that individuals and companies may apply for in the event of their becoming insolvent (unable to meet their liabilities and pay their creditors). The terminology might differ from territory to territory (technically only an individual can declare bankruptcy in the UK, for example, while businesses are either liquidated or go into administration), but the broad process is much the same.

Insolvency can strike for any number of reasons—an individual may amass unwieldy debts as the result of out-of-control spending or because an investment has turned bad. Businesses, meanwhile, go insolvent for two primary reasons:

they either lack sufficient assets to carry on trading, or they do not have sufficient cashflow to pay what they owe. A firm might find itself in such an unenviable situation perhaps as a result of bad management, a collapsing market for their product, or through simple bad luck. A farmer whose crops are destroyed by flooding, for instance, need hardly blame themselves for their plight.

the mechanics of bankruptcy

Typically, once an entity has been declared bankrupt (a status achieved by filing the relevant legal papers), the debtor's total assets are evaluated. They are then used to pay off a percentage of the debtor's obligations. By definition, the total assets will be worth less than the total debts, so a deal may be struck with creditors by which they agree to accept only a portion of what they are owed (on the basis that getting something back is better than getting nothing) in return for writing the remaining debt off. Often there is a legal hierarchy of creditors, usually beginning with company employees and the tax man.

Historically, most commercial bankruptcies have focused on distributing existing assets to creditors while winding up the failed business. As previously mentioned, even such brilliant business brains as Henry Ford have declared bankruptcy. But there is now an understanding that it can be in everyone's interests to help an entrepreneur get back on their feet. Thus there has been a move toward restructuring businesses (often under the supervision of a legally appointed administrator) so that they can continue trading and eventually find their way back to profit. This is a particularly common route for businesses declaring bankruptcy because of a cashflow problem.

Few of us relish the idea of going bankrupt, but it does allow the indebted entity (whether an individual or a business) to address their financial problems and plan for a brighter future. Once the bankruptcy process has played out in its entirety, the debtor is relieved of all their obligations and liabilities accrued prior to the declaration of bankruptcy. However, that is not to say that bankruptcy represents an easy way out. A bankrupt is likely to find it very difficult to secure credit for many years after their declaration, thus ruling them out of the property market, for example. Furthermore, those involved in commercial bankruptcies may find themselves banned from holding certain professional offices for a fixed period of time.

Bankruptcy, then, is a painful and undesirable experience. However, whereas once bankrupts may have faced an uncertain future in the poorhouse, in these more enlightened times it can mark a fresh start.

what was the Lehman Brothers' moment?

The biggest corporate bankruptcy in history occurred in September 2008 when the Lehman Brothers bank collapsed. Lehman Brothers was a staple of the global banking scene with a heritage going back to 1850. However, in the 21st century it became dangerously involved in the subprime-mortgage business. As the cracks in the U.S. property market grew from 2007, all Lehman Brothers' attempts to strengthen its underlying position failed. By the time it filed for bankruptcy (after desperate talks of a takeover came to nothing), the bank had debts in excess of $600 billion. An estimable American institution—the fourth-largest investment bank in the U.S. at the time—was wiped out overnight.

Aside from the sheer, jaw-dropping scale of the bankruptcy, the Lehman Brothers collapse was hugely symbolic. Its demise has come to be known as "the Lehman Brothers' moment"—the incident which made it absolutely clear that the U.S. economy (and, by extension, the global economy)—was careering into a financial crisis of the like not witnessed for decades. If Lehman Brothers could fall, no one was safe. In just a month following the collapse, some $10 trillion in market capitalization was wiped from the global equity markets. Rarely has a single bankruptcy had such a far-reaching impact.

giving it away

Charitable giving and philanthropy have existed for as long as society itself, but never have so many major organizations operated in a field now worth billions every year. Giving is big business.

It is worth establishing what we mean by the terms "charity" and "philanthropy." Charity has often been associated with alleviating the symptoms of a problem, while philanthropy tends more to addressing its root cause. To put it another way, to give a hungry man a fish is charity but to give him a rod and teach him to fish is philanthropy. There is also the question of scale: we tend to think of small donations as acts of charity and larger gifts as examples of philanthropy.

That is not to demean charity—there is much evidence to suggest that the most generous benefactors in terms of proportion of wealth given—come from the least wealthy sections of society. All those smaller contributions combine to fund work that truly changes lives. Nonetheless, in brutal economic terms, one eager and wealthy philanthropist can cover the ground of thousands of lower-level contributions.

Most of us who give to charity pass money on to a recognized charitable or non-profit organization, which then utilizes the money as it sees fit. The philanthropist, however, may opt to make a donation to a third-party organization or decide to establish an endowment, a gift administered by a charity or non-profit organization for a specific purpose. Alternatively, they can choose to establish a foundation of their own, which oversees specific projects in accordance with their wishes. The most high-profile example of this approach is the Gates Foundation, which maintains reserves worth tens of billions of dollars (see box far right).

While the altruistic nature of philanthropy should never be underestimated, there can be a financial incentive to giving as well. Most commonly, charitable giving brings tax breaks, so that donations may be written off against taxable income, reducing the donor's marginal cost of giving. That is to say, if someone gives $10 to charity and doesn't have to pay tax on it at a rate of, say, 15%, they are actually only "losing" $8.50 to the charity as the other $1.50 would have gone to the taxman anyway. And, if they face a tax rate of 45%, their donation only costs them $5.50. Thus governments can employ tax incentives to encourage a fairer distribution of wealth.

how do you mix business and charity?

The decades since the 1970s have witnessed the rise of social entrepreneurship, a form of business that uses classic market-based strategies to achieve socially minded goals. Rather than relying on donations or grants, as traditional charities and not-for-profits do, a social enterprise uses the profits it makes on the open market to meet a social need. Social enterprises take many different forms, from businesses offering employment opportunities to the socially disadvantaged through to fair-trade businesses seeking to fairly recompense farmers in the developing world. Social enterprises by their nature tend toward innovation. Consider, for example, SIRUM, an organization set up in 2009 by a group of Stanford University students. It redistributes unused, unexpired medicines (a commodity worth an estimated $5 billion per year) to low-income patients in the U.S. who wouldn't otherwise be able to afford them. By making it more economically desirable to recycle unwanted medicines than to destroy them, SIRUM ensures a valuable resource is exploited and a social need met, while turning a profit that allows its work to be ongoing. Essmart is another enterprising organization that sells life-improving technologies, such as solar lanterns and non-electric water filters, to poor areas of India via local sales agents. Such smart business models offer hope of a better future to millions.

the giving pledge

In terms of reconfiguring the philanthropic landscape, there may be no more significant initiative than the Giving Pledge campaign, championed by Bill Gates along with his wife Melinda and sometimes-richest-man-in-the-world, Warren Buffett. Targeting billionaires (or would-be billionaires were it not for their existing charitable giving), those who sign up to the pledge agree to giving away 50% or more of their wealth to good causes. As of January 2015, there were reportedly 128 signatories to the pledge, suggesting a philanthropic windfall of many billions to come.

economics is everywhere

Gary Becker, a leading figure in behavioral economics, employed economic approaches to examine questions that have traditionally been the preserve of other branches of the social sciences.

Gary Becker believed that we are rational consumers who conduct cost-benefit analyses to maximize our utility. His great leap was to consider how cost-benefit analyses guide decision-making in areas which economists had traditionally left alone, including crime, addiction, race and sexual discrimination, and family organization. He also did pioneering work in the field of human capital, establishing the now well-accepted notion that education is an investment in human capital.

Becker adopted a broad definition of utility that extended well beyond mere financial well-being, also taking account of, among other things, altruistic motivations and personal taste. His work has not always made for comfortable reading, as he assessed how we coolly weigh the economic advantages and disadvantages in making all sorts of sensitive life choices. For instance, in the 1950s he looked at the economics of discrimination in employment, establishing a now widely acknowledged truth that discrimination (which may provide utility by satisfying the personal preferences of the discriminator) nonetheless tends to incur a financial cost for the discriminator, and increasingly so the more competitive the industry in question is.

why do we do what we do?

Becker similarly applied cost-benefit analysis to address such questions as how far one interest group can exploit another within a democracy, why people take drugs, and why they commit crime. In regard to the last, he argued that, while crime might result from mental frailty or a confluence of social pressures, much of it relies on the perpetrator assessing that the potential gains to be made outweigh the potential losses if caught and punished. Comprehension of an economic imperative behind crime has had significant implications for public policy on both policing and justice.

But some of his most ground-breaking work was in the field of family economics. Along with Jacob Mincer at New York's Columbia University, he developed the so-called New Home Economics, and few of Becker's conclusions were designed to warm the hearts of romantics. For example, he looked at how economic considerations influence partner-matching in the marriage market (and also play a pivotal role in the divorce market), how self-interest inspires family members to help each other (epitomized by the so-called rotten kid theorem), how raising a child is an investment against the vagaries of old age, and how rising wages increase the opportunity cost for women who stay at home to raise a family. Furthermore, his study of family dynamics has helped to increase our understanding of, among other things, why fertility rates fluctuate and how welfare payments can impact the wider economy.

Becker's application of economic theory into sociological areas was revolutionary in its day but is now a well-established part of the mainstream. As he once told an audience at the University of Chicago:

> "My teachers taught me that economics was not a game played by clever academics but a serious subject that helped us understand the real world we lived in."

Gary Becker

Gary Becker was born in Pennsylvania in 1930. He graduated from Princeton in 1951 and received his doctorate from the University of Chicago four years later, with his thesis on racial discrimination. He married Doria Slote in 1954. In 1957 he took up a teaching post at Columbia University. In 1968 he moved to the University of Chicago, where he remained for over four decades. Considered a part of the Chicago School, Becker also joined the Mont Pèlerin Society cofounded by Milton Friedman in the 1940s. Becker's wife died in 1970, and, a decade later, he married Guity Nashat, a fellow academic. Among his works are *The Economics of Discrimination* (1957), *An Economic Analysis of Fertility* (1960), *Human Capital: A Theoretical and Empirical Analysis, with Special Reference to Education* (1964), *A Theory of the Allocation of Time* (1965), *A Treatise on the Family* (1981), and *Accounting for Tastes* (1996). He was awarded the 1992 Nobel Prize "for having extended the domain of microeconomic analysis to a wide range of human behavior and interaction, including nonmarket behavior." He said in his Nobel lecture: "The economic approach I refer to does not assume that individuals are motivated solely by selfishness or gain. It is a method of analysis, not an assumption about particular motivations... Behavior is driven by a much richer set of values and preferences." He died in Chicago in 2014.

how do national economies function?

measuring the economy

following orders

let spontaneous order rule

making the best of things

go with the flow

the banks' bank

more or less

monetarism

paying the man

balancing the books

labor

collective bargaining

labor pains

national debt

what's it worth?

measuring the economy

In order to be able to guide economic policy, governments strive to measure their economies as a whole. But the task of assessing an entity as complex as an economy is fraught with complications.

Doubtless the best-known measure in wide use is Gross Domestic Product (GDP)—the total market value of all goods and services produced in a country (or economic bloc) within a fixed time span (typically a year). GDP may be expressed in terms of the economy as a whole or on a per capita basis.

An alternative to GDP is Gross National Product (GNP), which expresses the total market value of all goods and services produced by the citizens of a given country (regardless of their location) within a fixed time span. While GDP includes production by foreign citizens working in a country, GNP measures the productivity of a country's own citizens only, whether based at home or abroad. Both measures can be expressed in nominal or in real terms. Nominal GDP is the sum of production expressed at current prices, while real GDP uses constant prices from a base year. Real GDP is therefore often regarded as a more accurate measure of economic progress.

getting the full picture

Both GDP and GNP should be used in conjunction with other indicators to gain a fuller picture of a country's economic health. For instance, the trade balance (the value of exports against imports), the national debt, the current account deficit, unemployment, and inflation all cast a light on how well an economy is doing.

Some experts seek an entirely different measure of economic prosperity. One is U.S. economist Richard Easterlin, who published a study in 1974 that saw little relationship between GDP and people's levels of reported happiness. What is the point of a robust economy if it does not increase the well-being of those living within it? It was a view backed in a 2007 report commissioned by the French government from a notable team of economists including Amartya Sen, Joseph Stiglitz, and Jean-Paul Fitoussi. They urged a shift in economic-policy focus away from simple measures of production to more nuanced measures of well-being that factored in life expectancy and measures of environmental sustainability as well as levels of reported happiness.

what are the BRICS?

For decades, the U.S. has topped the rankings of the world's biggest single-state economies as rated by GDP. Few would argue this is anything other than an accurate reflection of the U.S.'s position within the world. However, the fastest-growing major economy of recent times has been China, which is now the world's second-largest economy (having overtaken Japan) and is predicted by many to take over the top spot from the U.S. in the coming years. China is one of five nations that make up the so-called BRICS group of fast-growing major economies, along with Brazil, Russia, India, and South Africa. The group has held formal summits every year since 2009 to promote commercial, cultural, and political cooperation. While these nations were for a long time the poor relations of the traditional economic giants from North America and Europe, together they now account for some 40% of the global population and 20% of GDP. To put it another way, they are a force to be reckoned with and look set to reconfigure the global economic landscape over the next few decades. For economists, the success of the BRICS nations represents a seismic shift in global power and influence, although critics point to the huge disparities in wealth distribution within the BRICS that have seen millions miss out on the rewards of their respective commercial booms.

gross national happiness?

It seems that the tiny Himalayan kingdom of Bhutan has been ahead of the curve on this one. In 1972, its ruling monarch, Jigme Singye Wangchuck, called for an economy built not on Western ideals of materialism but on the country's traditional Buddhist values, a strategy he hoped would see GDP replaced by GNH (Gross National Happiness).

following orders

The free market may be the dominant economic model throughout the developed world, but it is not the only one. So, what are the alternatives?

The antithesis of the free-market economy is the centrally planned (or command) model. In a command economy, government, rather than businesses and consumers, drives economic activity through state-owned enterprises. The government decides everything from what is produced and in what quantities to how it is supplied, what it costs, and how it is consumed. Advocates of command economies (most notably, Karl Marx, see pages 66–7) argue that the state is better positioned to deliver social justice and equality, since wealth is not concentrated in the hands of a privileged minority as in a capitalist-market model.

The Soviet Union is the classic example of a command economy and illustrates many of its deficiencies. For instance, while command economies should, in theory, oversee the optimized use of resources in the public interest, they are prone to chronic inefficiency. This is because the absence of the free market removes many incentives for innovation, investment, and workplace efficiency. Furthermore, people's natural inclination to be greedy renders those in power susceptible to the temptation of directing resources toward themselves and their personal circle.

fundamental flaws

The pressures inherent in running every element within an economy are such that governments routinely fail to accurately record levels of demand and production and lack the ability to quickly respond to fluctuations on either side. As a result, regular shortages and surpluses—both examples of economic inefficiency—are commonplace in many command economies.

Meanwhile, a miscalculation in economic policy can have devastating consequences—such as when Stalin's dedication to industrialization led to a collapse of the agricultural sector that saw millions die of starvation. Stalin himself is a symbol of another of the system's weaknesses—a tendency toward autocratic leaders whose whims and ideological preferences carry excessive weight in economic-policy formulation. While the collapse of the USSR marked the end of command economies within Europe, several still operate, typically under communist regimes. Among them are Cuba and, perhaps most infamously, North Korea—a nation that echoes and even exceeds many of the worst failures of Stalinist Russia.

While pure command economies are becoming rarer, most nations should technically be described as mixed economies—that is to say, they combine elements of both the free market and the command economy, with private companies working alongside state-run operations. A variant of this is the social-market economy, which aims to blend the best of the free market with hand-picked elements of socialism—comprehensive welfare systems, for example. This was the model that has predominated in Western Europe for much of the period since World War II and provided the basis for West Germany's so-called economic miracle.

Hugo Chávez

Hugo Chávez breathed new life into the command-economy model during his tenure as Venezuelan president between 1999 and 2013. Rooted in socialist principles, his political philosophy came to be known as "Chavismo" and found widespread support in a South America tired of its perceived over-reliance on its North American neighbors. In a drive to bring much of the economy under government control, Chávez took over (or, at least, significantly regulated and increased state ownership) in sectors as disparate as agriculture, finance, gold, heavy industry, power, steel, telecommunications, tourism, and transport. But his most famous intervention was in the oil industry, as he sought to take advantage of the rising global oil price and Venezuela's vast oil reserves, the largest proven reserves in the world. With the resulting windfall revenues, he pushed through a program of social spending that made him a hero to many. Others, though, criticized him as autocratic and were suspicious of the cult of personality that grew up around him. In addition, while the oil industry boomed, other sectors, such as manufacturing, waned. His government's willingness to spend and its reluctance to save also left the country vulnerable to future economic shocks. Sure enough, many Venezuelans have subsequently reported shortages of staple goods, and Chávez's legacy remains ripe for debate.

let spontaneous order rule

As a leading figure of the Austrian School, Friedrich Hayek was one of the most influential economic voices of the 20th century—a dyed-in-the-wool supporter of the free market but a critic of mainstream economic orthodoxy.

The Austrian School is a wide-ranging school of economic thought, but it is broadly united by a belief that the free market, although imperfect, is best placed to allocate scarce resources. However, while the neoclassicists tend toward a model of the market in which rational players make informed decisions, the Austrian School contends that this system of perfect information exchange is a fiction. According to the likes of Hayek, it is because individual businesses and consumers are going about their self-interested way using information only of direct relevance to themselves that the free market should be left to its devices. The free market, they argue, is best equipped to assimilate all the information attached to every individual economic transaction and respond to it by supplying the goods and services demanded at the appropriate price—a process Hayek termed spontaneous order.

the road to serfdom

In an era when the theories of John Maynard Keynes (see pages 170–1) were becoming increasingly influential, Hayek took a diametrically opposed position, arguing that government intervention imperiled this spontaneous order. It was a thesis he explored most famously in his 1944 work, *The Road to Serfdom*. He believed that government intervention—guided at best by a small group of people and at worst by a single individual—could not begin to take account of the vast amount of information necessary to make wise economic choices. In Hayek's view, governments inevitably need to call on coercive techniques to impose their economic decisions. Furthermore, he contended, the less successful the government's strategies are, the more they rely on coercion so that society is drawn inexorably toward totalitarianism of the type then already being practiced by Hitler and Stalin.

Hayek was always a political theorist as much as an economist, with the two disciplines inevitably feeding into one another. Over time he honed his philosophy of what government should strive to do in economic terms. Essentially, he believed that the role of the state ought to be restricted to preserving the free-market mechanisms that allow for spontaneous order. To this end, the state can rightfully intervene to protect private property, enforce the legal status of contracts, and generally guard the rule of law, but he left little room for interference beyond that.

liberalism

As Keynesianism dominated the postwar economic landscape, Hayek and the Austrian School passionately argued against it, even where it didn't give rise to the authoritarian regimes Hayek feared. Despite being regarded as on the heterodox wing of economics, Hayek's work was co-opted— along with that of Milton Friedman and others—by the architects of the neoliberal economic consensus that overtook Keynesianism in the 1970s. Championed by Reagan's U.S. and Thatcherite Britain in the 1980s, the neoliberals subsequently dominated the global economic scene. As a kingpin of heterodox economics, Hayek thus came to exert mainstream influence that few could have predicted.

Friedrich Hayek

Friedrich Hayek was born in 1899 in Vienna. He fought on the Italian Front during World War I before studying at the University of Vienna, graduating in law in 1921 and political science in 1923. He then took a civil service job, where he encountered Ludwig von Mises, a prominent critic of socialism. Hayek was appointed director of the Austrian Institute for Business Cycle Research. His first book, *Monetary Theory and the Trade Cycle*, appeared in 1929. In 1932, he took up a professorship at the London School of Economics, becoming a UK citizen in 1938. During World War II he relocated with the LSE to Cambridge and, in 1942, published *The Pure Theory of Capital*. *The Road to Serfdom* followed in 1944 and *Individualism and Economic Order* in 1948. In 1947, he cofounded the Mont Pèlerin Society, dedicated to classical liberalism. In 1950, he left the LSE for the University of Chicago, where his research encompassed not only economics but also psychology, politics, and philosophy.

In 1962 Hayek moved to West Germany's University of Freiburg im Breisgau, retiring in 1968. In the 1970s he continued to publish and worked closely with a number of classic-liberal thinktanks. He shared the 1974 Nobel Prize with Swedish economist Gunnar Myrdal. Hayek's last book, *The Fatal Conceit*, was published in 1988. He died in Freiburg in 1992.

making the best of things

An average economy uses an awful lot of resources to produce a vast array of goods and services. So it makes sense to assess the optimum allocation of production resources—capital and labor, for example. Economists frequently refer to a graph known as the Production Possibility Frontier (PPF) to help with the task.

It should be the aim of an economy's leaders to move the economy onto—or, at least, as close as possible to—a spot on the PPF (see graph opposite). Exactly where on the arc they aim for depends on a nuanced consideration of wider needs. For the sake of simplicity, we will think in terms of an economy that produces only two things—in this case, socks and dog biscuits.

It is plain that the more socks that are produced, the fewer the resources that can be directed toward dog-biscuit production and vice versa. So the masters of this economy must decide just what ratio of resources to give to each product. If, for instance, the economy is in a tropical zone and has a high canine population, it makes sense to divert resources away from socks and toward dog biscuits. But, if the economy is based in the chilly North Atlantic and populated by animal-haters, production should doubtless be skewed toward socks and away from dog biscuits.

Alas, most real-world economies are rather more complicated. Nonetheless, the PPF is still a potent weapon in the economic arsenal when adapted to take account of the many production inputs and outputs available in a real economy. In the first place, government and society must reach a consensus on what to produce. This is a decision rooted not only in economic considerations but in political and social ones, too. As well as asking, "What can we produce most efficiently?" we must also consider what we value most—so, what proportion of our scarce resources do we allocate to defense, health, education, personal luxuries, etc.? Then we must consider any potential side effects—will, for example, producing a particular good critically degrade the environment? Once we know our basic basket of goods and services, we can then start to utilize the PPF.

what does the PPF look like?

The PPF works by illustrating all the maximum possible outputs for two (or more) products given a finite set of inputs. Here is a simple PPF for our land of socks and dog biscuits. The points A, B, and C show how increased production of one good necessitates lower production of the other. This arc is the PPF, and it is on this line that a fully efficient economy rests. Needless to say, there are very few of those about. Most economies actually lie somewhere to the left of the arc, as at point D. In such a case, the nation's resources are not being employed to their full potential. Point E, to the right of the arc, is unattainable, since it cannot be achieved with existing resources. Only an input of additional resources or more efficient means of production will allow for the economy to move to this point. Alternatively, an economic slowdown, war, or natural disaster can reduce production capacity and see a move to the left. However, under normal circumstances, the PPF for most economies will move in a rightward direction over the long term.

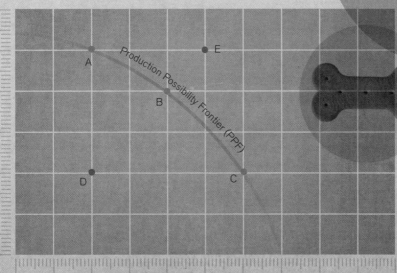

Socks Production

Production Possibility Frontier (PPF)

A

B

E

D

C

Dog Biscuits Production

go with the flow

Money maintains its value because there is a finite amount of it. Precisely how much is in circulation at any given moment profoundly impacts the state of the economy as a whole.

When we talk about money supply or money stock, we mean all the monetary assets within the economy at a particular time. There are a series of internationally accepted definitions, known as "M" classifications, for what constitutes monetary assets. M0—the baseline definition—comprises notes and coins together with the till money in banks and central-bank balances.

The money supply of a country is primarily controlled by the central bank (see page 120). The process of controlling supply is called monetary policy. There are four chief strategies available. First, the central bank can choose to print more money— often regarded as something of a desperate measure. Not only does it risk excessive inflation (see page 122) but it also does nothing to address any inherent problems within the economy.

Or the central bank can trade government bonds on the markets. By selling bonds and retaining the revenues, they can reduce the money supply, while by buying they release money into the system.

Alternatively, supply can be influenced by changing the interest rate. By raising the rate, credit becomes more expensive, ensuring that people are less keen to spend. The less they spend, the less money is in circulation. In contrast, lower the interest rate and credit gets cheaper, prompting increased consumer spending and a boost in money supply.

The fourth instrument that central banks can call upon is an adjustment to the reserve requirement of commercial banks. This is the proportion of deposits that a bank must hold back. The higher the reserve rate, the less the banks have to loan, forcing down money supply. Lower the reserve rate, and the effect is reversed.

why money supply matters

Additional money injected into the economy generally spurs economic activity. With more money in the system, credit gets cheaper and consumers have more of it to splash. As a result, businesses prosper and reinvest their profits, so increasing employment. In theory, the good times keep rolling on. However, increased demand, especially if it outstrips supply, pushes up prices. Banks respond by increasing interest rates, which slows consumer spending until the wheel turns full circle. Meanwhile, a reduction in money supply normally leads to a slowdown in economic activity, as there is less money to spend, raising the unhappy prospect of deflation (see page 122).

Money supply is also key to international trade. The more money there is, the more diluted the value of each unit—increased money supply gets you less bang for your buck. Lower money supply makes that buck more valuable. As money supply increases, therefore, importers see the value of their money reduce, meaning they can import less. Exporters, meanwhile, benefit, because their exports effectively become cheaper and more attractive to foreign markets.

Money supply is thus pivotal to the performance of an economy. As the doyen of bankers, Mayer Amschel Rothschild, once said:

> **"Give me control of a nation's money supply, and I care not who makes its laws."**

the cause of the "great moderation"

From the 1980s until the financial collapse of the late 2000s, the economy of the U.S. was unusually stable—a feature it shared with a good many other leading developed economies. GDP growth remained fairly constant, unemployment levels were less volatile than previously, and the inflation rate was pretty well contained. Ben Bernanke, a former chairman of the Federal Reserve, highlighted this trend in 2004, a phenomenon that had been dubbed the "great moderation" by U.S. economists James Stock and Mark Watson a couple of years earlier. Bernanke put down this prolonged period of economic calmness to a mixture of causes, including structural developments (such as financial deregulation and the use of technology in economic analysis), a reduction in the occurrence of unpredictable economic shocks, and sound macroeconomic policy.

A prominent feature of this last aspect, it was suggested, was better control of monetary policy, with knock-on impacts on employment, inflation, and the balance of trade. Of course, within four years the great moderation had given way to epic crisis, which rather undermined some of the argument. Nonetheless, economists continue to debate whether the great moderation was simply a historical anomaly or whether the powers-that-be really had got better at looking after the economy, including the notoriously prickly conundrum of how to regulate the money supply.

on monetary policy and is pivotal to controlling inflation.

- Set the base interest rate.
- Serve as the bank of the government.
- Maintain the nation's gold and foreign-exchange reserves.
- Serve as "lender of last resort," providing liquidity to commercial banks in times of crisis.
- Implement regulation across the industry.

game-changers

In order to fulfill their wide remit, central banks typically have an army of economists in close contact with both government and commercial institutions as they seek to navigate a steady economic course. Every decision a central bank makes, from injecting new money into the economy to changing interest rates, has an immediate repercussion as the markets react and then longer-term effects, influencing the inflation rate, the cost of credit, consumer spending patterns, and even the national mood.

The Bank of England is usually regarded as the first central bank, having been established in 1694 when the government of William III was desperate for loans to finance war with France. Creditors were attracted by the promise of being incorporated into the newly established Bank of England, which was granted privileges including the issuing of banknotes. However, it was not until the 20th century and the widespread demise of the gold standard—which, in turn, raised

the banks' bank

The central bank is the cornerstone on which a nation's entire banking system is typically built. How is it different from its fellow banking institutions?

A central bank is entrusted by its government to be the nation's central financial institution. Although generally "owned" by the government, many act with full autonomy. Central banks, which stand apart from the rest of the financial sector, are known as the Bank of Country Name—as in the Bank of England—but in the U.S., the central bank is called the Federal Reserve.

As implementer of monetary policy and overseer of the commercial-banking sector, a central bank is entrusted with an array of responsibilities. It will, for example:

- **Control the amount of money in circulation by issuing currency and trading government bonds. As such, it has the single biggest influence** the specter of uncontrolled inflation—that the central bank as we understand it today came to prominence.

Given that central banks wield vast power and influence, who keeps an eye on them? One such institution is the Bank for International Settlements, set up in 1930 with its headquarters in Basel, Switzerland. It was established in the aftermath of World War I to oversee the administration of monetary transfers outlined in the Treaty of Versailles. Today, it boasts a membership of some 60 leading central banks from countries representing about 95% of global GDP, and has a mission "to serve central banks in their pursuit of monetary and financial stability, to foster international cooperation in those areas, and to act as a bank for central banks."

should central banks be independent?

Most economists agree that central banks are best able to meet their myriad responsibilities when they are independent of both the government and commercial-banking interests. That is why many central banks, although technically owned by the government, operate at arm's length from the central administration.

In 1977, Finn Kydland and Edward Prescott (Norwegian and American, respectively) published a paper entitled "Rules Rather than Discretion." It investigated how the dual aims of low unemployment and low inflation represent a conflict of interest for most governments. Faced with rising unemployment, governments tend to increase the money in the economy to encourage job creation, which prompts a spike in demand and thus increases inflation. Kydland and Prescott noted that wily consumers will figure out that an increase in jobs will be accompanied by higher inflation. Consumers will therefore curb their spending in anticipation of rising prices and, as a result, nullify the hoped-for job surge, while inflation is likely to rise anyway as a result of excess money in the economy. Far better, the paper's authors said, to let monetary policy reside with a central bank more interested in controlling inflation than boosting employment. At the same time, the government's stated commitment to low inflation instantly becomes more credible.

more or less

As far as consumers are concerned, prices seem to rise far more often than they fall. But what do fluctuations in price mean for the wider economy?

A sustained increase in the general level of prices is called "inflation"; a general decline in prices is "deflation." Economists usually measure the rates of inflation and deflation on an annual basis, an important component in taking the pulse of an economy. This is typically done by comparing the relative prices of a basket of goods—that is, a preselected set of goods and services considered to reflect the broader economy.

not all inflation is bad

Inflation means that your money buys you less than it did, which is why individuals tend to dislike inflation. However, modest increases in inflation suggest a functioning economy with plenty of activity driven by demand. If your wages and pension increase at about the same rate as prices, you shouldn't be worse off. There are two major types of inflation:

- Demand-pull inflation—when demand is greater than supply, allowing suppliers to up the price.
- Cost-push inflation—when prices rise to cover increasing costs on the production and supply side.

The problems with inflation begin if it starts rising in an uncontrolled way. If prices rise unpredictably, consumers hold back on their spending—especially those whose incomes do not rise in line with inflation. High inflation also means that a country's exports become more expensive and so less popular. Too high inflation thus negatively impacts economic activity as a whole.

Hyperinflation describes a raging inflation rate—say, over 50% month-on-month. Such instability suggests major underlying problems and is often accompanied by social discord, unemployment, and shortages. A striking recent example of hyperinflation occurred in Zimbabwe, where the rate exceeded 230 million percent in 2008.

Disinflation is a fall in the rate of inflation which, if too steep, might suggest that a nation's economic health is in decline. We may enjoy lower prices for a while, but disinflation can hit businesses, raising the threat of increased unemployment, falling wages, and debt default. Deflation, meanwhile, increases all these risks.

more than your job's worth?

In the 1950s, New Zealand economist Bill Phillips argued that there was a direct correlation between inflation and employment. Using almost a century's worth of data from the UK, he argued that as unemployment decreases, inflation goes up and vice versa. It seemed suppliers responded to rising prices by upping supply and so increasing employment, adding more money into the economy that further pushed up prices. When people lost their jobs, however, money left the economy and so prices fell. But if governments thought they might be able to influence employment levels by tinkering with the inflation rate, they were soon disabused of the idea. In the U.S. in the 1970s, the relationship Phillips outlined appeared to have collapsed, as both inflation and unemployment went on the march, a scenario termed "stagflation."

Echoing Kydland and Prescott's conclusions (see page 121), Milton Freidman (see page 125) suggested that the problem was that people short-circuited the Phillips model by changing their behavior in expectation of inflation rises. If a government looks to boost economic activity by spending more money itself, consumers anticipate prices will rise. They therefore demand higher wages, which stymies employment growth while supporting inflationary trends. Friedman thus suggested that governments ought not to try to manipulate market demand by undertaking spending programs in order to bring down unemployment.

monetarism

Milton Friedman was the architect of monetarism, which enjoyed its heyday in the 1970s and 1980s. Monetarists believe that governments should interfere in the economy little more than to control the money supply.

Monetarism has its roots in the quantity theory of money. According to this theory, which originated in the 16th century:

$MV = PT$, where M = the amount of money in circulation over a defined time period, V = the velocity of money (that is, how often it is spent in that period), P = the average price level, and T = volume of transactions.

Experience shows that V tends to remain reasonably constant in the long run, so that increases in M lead to increases in P. That is to say, the more money there is in the economy, the higher prices rise in the long term. According to monetarism, keep a tight rein on money supply, and the markets will look after inflation and unemployment.

In the 1950s, Friedman took on the Keynesian hypothesis that private individuals tailored their consumption to reflect their current income, instead arguing that consumers cast a distinction between their secure, long-term permanent income and shorter-term, less stable transitory income. The former, he suggested, was more important to consumption patterns over the long term. Whereas government expenditure might temporarily boost transitory income, controlling money supply was a surer way to exert a predictable influence on long-term incomes and, by extension, expenditure, he said.

let the markets do their job

Friedman also cast doubt on the long-held notion that governments could lower unemployment by increasing government spending if they were prepared to accept the pay-off of rising inflation. Friedman instead argued that, as prices increase, workers demand higher wages, leading to employers cutting jobs. Rather than facing a choice between either high unemployment or high inflation, Friedman said that an economy could be stuck with both—a theory borne out by the stagflation (persistent high inflation alongside high unemployment) suffered by the U.S. economy in the 1970s.

Furthermore, where Keynes highlighted the inherent instability of markets,

Friedman, conversely, emphasized their long-term stability given the right circumstances. According to Friedman, the real reason that the Great Depression occurred was because the Federal Reserve excessively tinkered with money supply, allowing it to fall by too much. Friedman contended that in the short run, increased supply of money prompts increased output and employment, while decreased supply does the opposite. Over the long term, meanwhile, increased monetary growth causes prices to rise but has little impact on overall output.

Government, therefore, he suggested, best serves the needs of the economy simply by ensuring there is sufficient money supply in the system to meet consumer demand for it—for this purpose, Friedman treated money as a good that embodied purchasing power. The demand for new money, he argued, was broadly predictable, and, once satisfied, the free market is best placed to keep inflation and unemployment in check. He contended that central banks should thus increase money supply roughly in line with GDP growth.

Monetarism became the dominant macroeconomic philosophy in many of the leading industrialized nations during the 1970s and 1980s. However, monetarism did not bring an end to economic downturns any more than Keynesianism had. Instead, it is now more commonly employed as part of a multifaceted approach to macroeconomic management.

Milton Friedman

Milton Friedman was born in New York in 1912 to Jewish parents recently arrived from the Austro-Hungarian Empire. In 1932, he graduated in math and economics from Rutgers University in New Jersey and received a masters from the University of Chicago a year later. From the mid-1930s to the mid-1940s, he worked mostly in public service. In 1938, he married Rose Director. He earned his doctorate from Columbia in 1946 and the same year moved to the University of Chicago, remaining for some 30 years and becoming a lynchpin of the Chicago School of economics. His published output included *A Theory of the Consumption Function* (1957), *Capitalism and Freedom* (1962), *A Monetary History of the United States, 1867–1960* (1963; written with Anna Schwartz), and *The Role of Monetary Policy* (1968).

Friedman was awarded the Nobel Prize in 1976. He retired from the University of Chicago the following year and forged links with the Hoover Institution at Stanford. Friedman became arguably the key economic advisor to the Reagan government in the 1980s, advocating minimal state intervention. His book *Free to Choose* was immensely popular, and he was an in-demand commentator for the rest of his life. He died in San Francisco in 2006. *The Economist* described him as "the most influential economist of the second half of the 20th century... possibly of all of it."

paying the man

If you find taxes taxing, take heart: no lesser intellect than Albert Einstein once declared: "The hardest thing in the world to understand is the income tax."

A tax is a compulsory payment to a government that may be levied against an individual or a business. Few of us enjoy paying taxes, but without them our governments would simply cease to operate.

The effectiveness of a tax system is measured by economists in terms of how tax revenues affect the efficient and equitable allocation of resources. A government should aim to generate sufficient funds through the tax system to be able to carry out its various obligations while keeping the tax burden—the total cost to a country of paying taxes—as low as possible. The tax burden includes not only the cost of the taxes themselves but also the costs incurred in collecting them, administering the tax system, and ensuring all tax-payers comply with the regulations. In addition, the burden takes account of the deadweight cost—losses incurred in the market as a result of distortions that arise when consumers and suppliers have to set aside a portion of their expenditure for taxes.

what's yours is theirs

Taxes can, in principle, be levied on pretty much anything, but here below is a selection of the main types:

- **Income tax**—a tax on income, often levied at different rates depending on the size of the income.
- **Sales tax**—levied on goods and services purchased by businesses and private individuals.
- **Property tax**—levied against both private and commercial real estate. These are often one-time-only taxes paid, for instance, at the time of purchasing a property.
- **Corporate tax**—paid by businesses on the basis of income. Tax levels vary depending on the structure of a company.
- **Payroll tax**—a tax on wage payments incurred by employees, employers, and the self-employed. The amount is usually a set percentage of wages.
- **Capital gains tax**—paid when investments are cashed in.
- **Death duties**—for more on inheritance and estate taxes see page 100.

Taxes are described as progressive when those most able to pay (the rich) are charged a greater proportion. Take income tax as an example. Those below a certain level of earnings may typically pay the tax at a lower level (say, 10%) or be exempted altogether, while those within an average earning bracket pay more (20% perhaps) and those above a certain threshold pay a still higher rate (40% or more). By contrast, taxes such as VAT are flat-rate, payable at the same level regardless of personal circumstances.

Most would agree that it is socially equitable for the wealthy to pay a greater share of taxes, although this is not unproblematic. Put too great a burden on the rich (often the most successful entrepreneurs within an economy) and they may relocate themselves and their businesses elsewhere to enjoy a more generous tax regime. Not only does the government miss out on the émigré's future tax revenues but it also risks losing a business that provides employment to others.

evading or avoiding?

While it is true that the rich pay a disproportionate share of the taxes in many developed countries—in the UK, for instance, the richest 1% of earners pay somewhere between a quarter and a third of the total income-tax take)—it is also widely acknowledged that the wealthy are best placed to exploit tax loopholes by, for example, paying accountants to arrange their finances in the most beneficial way. Arranging your affairs in such a manner as to reduce the amount of tax you pay is known as tax avoidance. Tax avoidance is legal, in contrast to tax evasion—failure to pay taxes owed as a result of filing a false tax return or no return at all. Methods of tax avoidance include establishing companies or subsidiary companies in offshore jurisdictions with lower tax rates, setting up shell companies—companies that have legal status but do not actively trade, serving instead as instruments through which to funnel money—and taking up residence in a tax haven, a country that attracts rich foreigners by offering a friendly tax environment. In practice, it can be difficult to distinguish the legal line between avoidance and evasion. Nonetheless, some argue that, while evasion is immoral, avoidance is entirely fair. It is sometimes claimed that accountants are, indeed, duty-bound to seek out innovative ways to reduce the tax burdens of their clients. Their critics, meanwhile, argue that they have a moral duty not to deprive the authorities of legitimate revenues.

balancing
the books

It is the job of government to provide an array of vital public goods and services that either the market would fail to deliver or which are too important to be left to the private sector.

Which goods and services should fall under the remit of the government is always up for debate. Should a government provide free healthcare for everybody at the point of delivery, as happens in the UK? Or should individuals be responsible for insuring themselves against health risks, as has historically happened in the U.S.? Such questions can lead to fraught debates.

Nonetheless, there is a basket of public goods common to a large proportion of governments around the world. It may typically include debt repayments, defense, education, enterprise, environment, foreign affairs, government, health, housing, international aid, local government, social welfare, sport, the arts, and transport.

Some of these, such as education, are regarded as so vital to a country's well-being that most governments take a stake in their provision. Schools, for example, could, in theory, be run exclusively by private organizations but a legally established state-education system increases the likelihood that all children receive at least a basic education and reduces the risk of the less wealthy being priced out of the system.

Other goods and services are provided where it is not practical for the private sector to do so. Streetlighting, for example, is a service enjoyed by everybody, but such is its nature that a private company would be unable to secure payment from all those who use it. With no possibility of making a profit, the market would simply cease to provide streetlights. Thus it falls to the government to provide the service.

a wide remit

As well as providing essential goods and services, governments may also support or subsidize a struggling industry—agriculture, for example, commonly receives state subsidies—or offset externalities (for instance, picking up the costs of dealing with diminished air quality or wear and tear to transport infrastructure).

The government's finances are maintained by treasuries, commonly known as ministries of finance. A treasury looks after the public purse, managing the

who should look after a nation's health?

Whose responsibility is healthcare? It is a question that came into sharp focus when President Barack Obama introduced historic reforms to the healthcare system of the U.S. in 2009. Up to that point, most Americans had been responsible for arranging their own health insurance, usually through their employers or through private providers. It was estimated by the U.S. Census Bureau in 2008 that over 46 million people were uninsured, so qualified for treatment in emergency rooms only, and a great many more were underinsured. Furthermore, Americans spent some 16.2% of GDP on healthcare—over twice the average of other OECD countries. Obama's scheme, nicknamed "Obamacare," aimed to secure insurance for the 15% of the population previously without it by offering subsidies to make it more affordable, as well as making larger employers responsible for providing schemes for their workers. A large part of the Republican opposition and the population as a whole stood firmly against the legislation, unhappy at the potential strain on public finances and the threat the reforms posed to jobs. Amid accusations of overbearing government interference from some quarters, Obamacare was introduced in 2010 but had to see off a series of legal challenges over the following few years.

Across the Atlantic, meanwhile, the UK population has enjoyed free healthcare at the point of delivery through the state-run National Health Service (NHS) since 1948. Indeed, the NHS is widely regarded as a national treasure. The comparison of the British and American systems thus highlights just one of the challenges a government faces in deciding how to spend the public purse.

too big to fail?

Having said that nationalization is not currently de rigueur in the developed world, it should be noted that the financial chaos of this century has seen a dramatic increase in government ownership within the banking sector. Governments around the world have been forced to step in to save (and, in some cases, take over) private institutions whose demise, it was argued, would cause unacceptable disruption to society as a whole. It is sometimes said that these privately held banks were simply "too big to fail." That so many were able to call on public money to offset their inefficiencies and excesses must rate as perhaps the single greatest episode of market failure in history.

The pattern for bank nationalization was set by Iceland, which effectively nationalized three of its biggest banks—Kaupthing, Landsbanki, and Glitnir—in 2008. By that point, the country's financial sector had assets far in excess of the national GDP, having accessed the international credit markets to underpin growth. As the global economy hit the rocks, there were serious doubts as to the Icelandic banks' abilities to meet their debt obligations. As the banks came under increasing pressure, the government had little option but to step in or risk the collapse of its entire economy. While staving off immediate disaster, the sorry series of events negatively impacted the economy for years and did little for the country's international standing.

government's revenues and distributing them in accordance with government policies and legal requirements. Public spending can be described either as current spending (spending that has to be regularly renewed—wages and raw materials, for example) or capital spending (long-term spending on physical assets such as hospital buildings and road infrastructure).

When a government spends more than its revenues in a given year, it is said to be running a deficit. When revenues outpace spending, there is a budget surplus. One argument is that it is acceptable to run a deficit if debt is kept in check and spending goes toward projects that stimulate wider economic growth. This was famously the opinion of John Maynard Keynes (see pages 170–1), whose opinions found renewed favor in light of the global slowdown of the late 2000s after years out of favor.

state of play
Most developed nations have large private sectors, but many include a few state-owned companies that were once privately owned. What drives the process of nationalization and its counterpart, privatization?

Nationalization is the process by which a government takes a privately owned business or industry into state ownership. The former private owners typically receive some form of compensation for their loss, although it is not uncommon in certain parts of the world for a regime to commandeer a business forcibly.

For the most part, the governments of the developed world accept that, for all its faults, the private sector and its profit-led businesses are best placed to provide most goods and services. However, there are good reasons for a process of nationalization:

- **An industry may operate as a natural monopoly (see page 79), so that state ownership becomes a way to moderate the potential excesses of a monopoly.**
- **A government may believe an industry should provide unprofitable services for the public good, which a private business would simply withdraw as financially unviable. For instance, postal services might be nationalized to ensure the provision of loss-making rural deliveries.**
- **A government may see the chance to exploit the profitability of a particular industry to bolster its revenues. For example, the discovery of significant mineral deposits might convince an administration to take the mining industry into public ownership.**
- **A vital industry deemed to be suffering from underinvestment and/or inefficient management may be ripe for nationalization. This is particularly the case for industries that demand heavy long-term investment, such as railways.**
- **A socialist government may be ideologically committed to reducing the influence of private capitalists, while correspondingly increasing government influence.**

- **There may be other exceptional circumstances. For instance, the U.S. government effectively nationalized airport security in the wake of the 9/11 attacks.**

into private hands

Privatization is the reverse process, by which a business or industry is taken from public to private ownership, typically through a share issue or by granting operating licenses. In some cases, it may be the ideological goal of a government committed to free-market economics. Alternatively, it can be a measure to rectify perceived inefficiencies that some believe are endemic in state-run operations—largely as a result of the lack of profit motive and through the inevitable politicization of the economic decision-making process—or to break up an industry that demonstrates unhealthy monopolistic tendencies. Privatization can also bring a welcome short-term surge of revenues to a government, while also removing a long-term drain on the state's finances.

After a trend among many countries, including the UK, toward nationalization for significant parts of the 20th century, since the 1980s there has been a concerted ideological move away from it in much of the developed world.

labor

Along with land and capital, labor is one of the three major factors of production. However, it is the only one made up of living, breathing people, making it a complex beast to tame.

The labor force is the total number of people of working age who are working or actively seeking work. They drive an economy, utilizing the other means of production to create new goods and services.

Labor is a supply-side resource, but, because workers are also consumers, the labor participation rate—the proportion of the labor force that is economically active—has a direct influence on the demand side. In a flourishing economy, increased demand leads to increased employment, which further swells demand as more workers have more money to spend. By contrast, weakening demand means less employment, with fewer workers with money to spend consolidating lower demand.

The labor market is the arena in which employees and employers meet to exchange labor for a wage and agree other conditions of work. The market works like any other in that it is guided by supply and demand—where labor is scarce, it is more expensive and vice versa. However, legally enforceable regulation—such as a minimum wage—can be implemented to ensure that workers' rights are observed. Around 90% of nations operate some kind of minimum-wage system. Nonetheless, unscrupulous employers can attempt to bypass such legislation by employing on an informal basis (see Under the Counter, page 154) or by recruiting workers from illegal sources (for instance, undocumented immigrants and children).

what work is worth

The wage that an employee may demand depends on a number of factors. These include: geography (Luxemburg has the world's highest average per capita—a term meaning for every person—salary, with Tajikistan officially having the lowest according to the International Labour Organization); education and training (typically, the better educated you are, the higher your earning capacity); age and experience (in the U.S., in 2011, the age group 45–54 was the highest-earning, followed by those aged 35–44); and the sector in which you want to work (the financial sector, for instance, is generally better remunerated than, say, the arts).

Adam Smith on labor

Adam Smith believed that a division of labor so that workers become specialized in a particular process was vital for economic efficiency. According to this theory, a bakery with three employees will make 150 loaves of bread more efficiently if Employee 1 makes the dough, Employee 2 kneads it, and Employee 3 bakes it, than if each employee makes 50 loaves each from scratch. This is because time is not wasted switching between tasks and because through repetition of a single task, each becomes increasingly efficient at it. However, the likes of Marx believed employer-imposed specialization threatened to dehumanize workers and trap them in repetitive and unsatisfying roles for the benefit of the employer. Marx also critiqued Smith's take on the labor theory of value.

According to Smith, the true value of a good is related to the labor used in its production or the labor it saves for its consumer. For Marx, however, that value should also take account of the labor involved in providing the resources needed to make a product. Thus, if a carpenter takes a day to build a chair and his daily wage rate is $150, the chair is worth $150 plus the cost of the wood (valued at, say, $50) plus the cost of any lost value to the carpenter's tools (valued, perhaps, at $2 on an original value of $100). In turn, the tools are valued to factor in the labor required to produce them plus the labor used to excavate the minerals from which they are made. In addition, the wood takes account of the labor of the forester who cut it plus the labor used in the creation of his tools.

work all hours?

Common sense suggests that the longer you work, the more productive you are and the more the economy as a whole benefits. However, the empirical evidence suggests otherwise. Although the economically advanced South Koreans work the longest hours on average in the world, relatively underdeveloped nations such as Chile, Bangladesh, and Sri Lanka are not far behind. Meanwhile, the countries with the shortest working-hour averages are the affluent Germany and the Netherlands. This is because the overall level of productivity is more important than the number of hours put in. An economy that can provide its workers with the technological equipment to best carry out their work requires less labor input than less technologically advanced nations.

collective bargaining

Beatrice Webb was a key figure in the development of the British trade-union movement in the late 19th and early 20th centuries. A champion of workers' rights, her writings had a profound influence on labor relations.

The idea of workers combining forces to protect their existing rights and fight for new ones has a long heritage in Europe, with craft guilds fulfilling that purpose for selected skilled professions since the medieval period. However, it was the Industrial Revolution and the emergence of the factory system in Britain—often characterized by low wages and poor working conditions—that brought into sharp focus the question of how workers could best protect their interests, while their employers were driven primarily by desire for profit.

The British government quickly outlawed the emerging trade unions that brought together workers for the purpose of representing them in negotiations with their bosses. For the first quarter of the 19th century, any worker found guilty of entering into a union with another in order to secure better working terms could be given a jail sentence. Unions were legalized in the UK from 1824 but were severely restricted in what actions they could take. Nonetheless, union membership rocketed in Britain and throughout Europe and later in the U.S., too. However, while their advocates argued that they played a vital role in protecting workers from potential exploitation, many in society—not least those who employed large numbers of workers—feared that trade unionism was a step along the path of social revolution advocated by the likes of Marx.

the national minimum

Beatrice Webb (née Potter) entered the fray in the 1880s when she assisted her relative, Charles Booth, in his ground-breaking study of the London poor. In 1891 she published a study of her own, *The Co-operative Movement in Great Britain*. It was now that she introduced the term "collective bargaining" to describe the process by which a trade union engages with employers (or an employers' association) to negotiate on issues including wages, working hours, job security, and other working conditions. With her husband, Sidney Webb, she also laid out terms for "a national minimum of civilized life," designed to ensure no worker would be allowed to fall below a minimum level of remuneration and quality of life.

Webb played a crucial role in making trade unionism respectable, using empirical data to explain how collective bargaining could contribute to social justice. Indeed, collective bargaining came to be seen as offering a boon to employers, too, since it significantly streamlined the process of agreeing terms of employment with large numbers of individuals. Furthermore, collective bargaining fed into the emerging economic philosophy that a happy labor force is more productive.

Critics of collective bargaining claim it artificially increases wages for union members while suppressing those of non-members and even imperiling jobs. Many trade unions have found their power diminished in recent decades through legislation drafted by governments wary of overpowerful unions that can inflict wide economic damage, especially by exercising the right to strike. Nonetheless, Webb played a vital role in rebalancing power between employers and workers.

Beatrice Webb

Beatrice Potter was born in 1858, in Gloucestershire, England, into a prosperous commercial family. Her grandfather had been a Liberal MP. Beatrice became interested in the causes of poverty and developed a fascination with the co-operative movement. After her work with Charles Booth and publication of *The Co-operative Movement in Great Britain*, she married Sidney Webb in 1892. Prominent members of the socialist Fabian Society, the couple worked together to produce the highly influential *The History of Trade Unionism* in 1894, followed by *Industrial Democracy* in 1897. In 1895, they were cofounders of the London School of Economics.

From 1905–9 she served on the Royal Commission on the Poor Laws and Relief of Distress. She produced a report that anticipated many aspects of the welfare state introduced after World War II. In 1913, the Webbs founded the *New Statesman* political journal. She assisted Sidney in the campaign that saw him elected Labour MP for Seaham in 1922. He remained in parliament until 1931, having held the positions of president of the board of trade and secretary of state for the colonies and dominion affairs. In the 1930s and 1940s the couple traveled to the USSR, producing *Soviet Communism: A New Civilisation?* (1935) and *The Truth About Soviet Russia* (1942), a book which critics have since accused of being dangerously uncritical. Beatrice died in 1943.

labor pains

Unemployment is the scourge of governments everywhere. How best to manage the problem—especially in a world where technological advances often lessen demand for labor—is a question that continues to divide economists and policy-makers.

Unemployment describes the situation where an individual is actively seeking employment but unable to find suitable work. An economy's unemployment rate is the percentage of the entire economically active population—those of working age who are fit and able to work—with no work despite actively seeking it.

High unemployment is indicative of an economy with problems. It generally occurs when economic activity is insufficient to support businesses recruiting and retaining staff. Furthermore, those who are unemployed are unable to contribute their productivity on the supply side and have less money to spend on the demand side, compounding the problem of slack economic activity. Where welfare benefits are paid to those out of work, unemployment acts as a drain on the state's finances. Most governments aim for a situation of full employment—a state of equilibrium in which all those who want to work at the going wage are employed— but none entirely succeed. Nor would it be desirable, it is argued by some economists, given that high inflation often goes hand in hand with low unemployment.

categories of unemployment

- **Classical—when real wages mean that the cost of employing a worker is higher to an employer than the benefit gained from employing them.**
- **Cyclical—which sees unemployment grow as an economy enters a downturn in the "natural cycle" of boom and bust.**
- **Frictional—unemployment that occurs as employees enter the job market or transfer between jobs. It occurs as workers wait to be matched to a suitable post rather than the first one available, a process that may be delayed by a lack of resources or information on either the employee's or employer's side. Frictional unemployment is considered inevitable, even when there is near full employment.**
- **Marxian— Marx argued that capitalist employers are incentivized to maintain a certain level of unemployment, since**

unemployment creates competition in the labor market that keeps wages low.

- Seasonal—owing to lack of demand for a particular good or service at certain times of the year.
- Structural—the result of large-scale trends and changes in the economy. For instance, workers may lack the skills to find employment in emerging new industries or be geographically distant from a region where jobs are available. Structural unemployment occurs where there is a mismatch between what employers require and what employees can provide.

Many economists, including Milton Friedman, believe there is a natural rate of unemployment, which occurs in a non-inflationary environment as a result of supply-side factors only, such as frictional and structural unemployment.

willing to work?

What can and should a government do to help alleviate unemployment? According to classical economics, the market will ensure a state in which all who want to work can and therefore unemployment is a choice in that it is always possible to find a job if you will work for lower wages.

Until the end of the 19th century, there was a consensus that unemployment was the fault of the individual— either an unwillingness or an inability to work. But, as the 20th century got underway, it became clear that a good deal of unemployment was involuntary, so that even workers willing to work for the going wage could not find a job. Many economists argued that the major problem was with the high level of workers' real wages (the purchasing power of a wage taking inflation into consideration). In short, workers needed to accept lower wages to ensure higher employment. However, John Maynard Keynes offered a radically different interpretation against the backdrop of the Great Depression and the mass unemployment of the 1930s. He argued that neither workers nor businesses could solve the problem by wage moderation, since wages are "sticky" and fall more slowly than prices. In other words, when recession hits and demand falls, real wage value increases, causing higher unemployment. Instead, he believed government spending could kick-start the economy and create more jobs (see Keynesianism, page 170).

national debt

The world is seriously in debt—the combined liabilities of governments amount to over $50 trillion, almost $8,000 for every person on the planet. Remarkably, it is the developed world that is most in the red.

National debt is the total debt owed by a country's government, both to its own citizens (internal debt—accounting for the majority of national debt) and to foreign creditors (external debt). It may also be called government debt, public debt, or sovereign debt. National debt is a long-term means of financing government operations and has become increasingly prevalent over recent decades.

Some governments turn to organizations such as the IMF and the World Bank for credit, but robust economies usually raise loans by issuing securities—government bonds, for example. These may be bought by individuals, institutions or other governments and offer a regular interest payment before full redemption on a given date. They are, historically, regarded as low-risk, since governments have traditionally been able to meet debt obligations by raising taxes, through the natural expansion of the economy, or (in a worst-case scenario) by printing more money.

In addition, since most government debt is internal debt, there is an assumption that creditors will generally come to an accommodation with a government struggling to meet its liabilities since, under normal circumstances, the creditors' wider economic interests demand government stability. Therefore, many governments are happy to bear a certain level of debt. It is notable that the countries with the biggest national debts today are all generally regarded as developed countries. For instance, according to *Forbes* magazine, in 2014 Japan had by far the highest level of government debt (at nearly 230% of GDP), while the next five most indebted countries included Singapore, the U.S., and three European nations.

unsustainable debt

That said, the experience of the current century grimly illustrates the dangers of spiraling government debt burdens. If the debt begins to get out of control, citizens can expect one or more unwelcome outcomes: higher taxes, rising inflation, political instability, and social discontent. The debt crisis that began in Greece in 2009, for example, is likely to serve as a case study in the dangers of national debt for decades to come. A toxic combination of long-term low tax revenues and high expenditure first saw Greece on the brink of default in 2010, before the IMF and European Central Bank granted loans worth tens of billions of euros to stave off immediate collapse. In return, and with its future within the eurozone at risk, Greece was compelled to undertake a program of stringent austerity that led to widespread rioting, brought down the incumbent government, and caused severe hardship for significant portions of the population.

unpopular ratings

Just as for individuals who suffer debt problems, countries that have been unable to meet their obligations face problems securing credit in the future. The credit-worthiness of nations is decided by credit-ratings agencies—the big three in the field are Fitch, Moody's and Standard & Poor. A reduction in a country's credit rating indicates a greater likelihood of default. Greece's credit rating, unsurprisingly, slumped during its debt crisis, yet even the U.S.—long-time holders of the highest classification—had its rating marginally reduced on the back of the credit crunch, with the UK suffering a similar fate in 2013.

why wipe the slate clean?

While rich countries have tended to build the biggest debt obligations, it has historically been poorer countries with more modest liabilities who have suffered most under their burdens. According to the World Bank, the combined debt of developing nations reached $4 trillion in 2010, an increase of more than 10% in a single year. As the new century dawned, it was clear that national debt was strangling the prospect of development across swathes of the globe, especially in sub-Saharan Africa. Leading economists such as Jeffrey Sachs argued for canceling the debt in selected countries—the IMF and World Bank identified some 40 nations termed "heavily indebted poor countries" (HIPCs) that were eligible for debt relief—so spurring economic development in the recipient countries and reducing their ongoing reliance on international aid. Others felt the West had a moral duty to strike bad debts from the book, since the World Bank and other institutions had an unfortunate track record of granting loans to corrupt regimes that did not use the money for the intended purposes.

Amid a wave of popular support, the G8 countries—an informal grouping of eight of the world's leading economies—agreed to write off some $40 billion of debt in 2005. Few predicted that it would be Europe facing the world's greatest debt crisis within just five years.

what's it worth?

As any traveler will know, money comes in many different currencies and denominations (that is, units of value). But why do currencies matter, and how do they relate to each other?

Currency includes all the money issued by an authority and in general use in a particular country or economic area. In the U.S., it's the dollar, in the UK it's the pound sterling, in Japan it's the yen, and across most of the European Union it's the euro.

The first known coin-based currency was in operation around 600 BCE, although trade tended to be localized. There were, though, exceptions—the Romans operated a notably successful single currency across their vast empire. Over the centuries, a huge array of local currencies took root as nations asserted their own identity and influence This led to problems for traders of different areas: how did they know what their currencies were worth relative to each other? It made no

sense to trade a unit of Currency A for one of Currency B if an A bought you a slice of bacon while a B got you a whole pig in their respective markets.

The solution was to hit upon a common measure of value. Gold was ideal—it was widely valued and in finite supply. At first gold was physically exchanged, but, precious metal being unwieldy to transport, traders exchanged their respective currencies on the basis of their respective values relative to that of gold, the so-called gold standard. Governments agreed to peg the creation of new currency to the volume of gold they possessed—and a system of foreign exchange developed.

from gold bars to dollar bills

This system prevailed into the 20th century, with the currency exchange rates—the value of one currency relative to another—decided either by agreement between the relevant governments or determined by the markets. Since the end of World War II, the U.S. dollar has largely replaced gold as the standard marker of value on account of its long-term stability. Today, trading in foreign exchange is a huge business—some $2 trillion is traded daily as traders look to profit from deviations in exchange rates over a given time period. For instance, you might buy a quantity of pounds sterling at $1.56 apiece in the morning and sell them at $1.58 in the evening. On a $100,000 investment, that represents a healthy profit of almost $1,300.

what is a currency crisis?

A "currency crisis" occurs where one currency experiences a sudden steep collapse in its value relative to other currencies. Such crises have become more common since the 1970s and the widespread demise of the gold standard (see page 95). Two of the worst occurred in the 1990s: Latin America in 1994 and Asia in 1997.

Currency crises are difficult to predict but most likely to occur where a government has borrowed heavily and investors are nervous as to what that government is going to do next. Faced with a declining exchange rate, a government may try to prop its currency up by selling foreign-exchange reserves and retaining the domestic currency received. Reducing the domestic currency in circulation increases demand, and the exchange rate rises. However, this is a short-term strategy with many negative effects, including the threat of higher unemployment. Alternatively, a government may look to devalue the currency—lower its value relative to other currencies—to make exports cheaper and imports more expensive, so reducing trade imbalances and increasing employment. Either way, investors get jittery about the economy's prospects and move their money into safer havens abroad.

This process, known as "capital flight," worsens exchange rates as international markets are flooded with "cheap" currency for sale, aggravating economic conditions in the domestic economy. So a crisis can spiral into a disaster, often given added momentum by traders betting on the crisis worsening.

foreign exchange

Foreign exchange—known as Forex or FX—tends to be an expensive and fiddly business. So why don't we all share a single currency? Primarily, because having a local currency gives a government greater influence over its country's economic circumstances. Nonetheless, the European Union adopted the euro virtually in 1999 (with coins and notes coming into circulation in 2002) in the greatest single-currency experiment in history. Cyberspace, meanwhile, has the bitcoin.

how do international economies function?

the global market

comparative advantage

a protective arm

one big family

dependency theory

under the counter

in development

raising the bar

entitlement theory

big beasts

6

the global market

Take a wander around your local shops and you will soon see how international trade impacts all our lives—from the car you drive to the oil you put in it and the coffee you drink.

International trade describes the exchange of goods and services between nations. The goods and services a country sells abroad are exports, and those it buys in are imports. International trade allows, theoretically, for more efficient use of a country's economic resources, since it allows nations to focus on producing what they are best equipped to produce, while turning to trading partners for the things it can't produce efficiently (see Comparative Advantage page 146).

International trade also breeds economic networks, encouraging, say, Foreign Direct Investment (FDI), whereby residents of one country buy assets or business interests in another. FDI injects capital into the recipient country and typically creates jobs, benefiting the host country's wider economy. Meanwhile, for the investor, FDI represents an opportunity to benefit from the growth of a business from which they might otherwise be excluded.

The balance of trade is the difference between a country's imports and exports. Where exports exceed imports, the country runs a trade surplus; where imports are larger than exports, it is called a trade deficit. In this calculation, exports include foreign-aid outflows, domestic consumer spending abroad (by tourists, for example), and domestic investments abroad. Imports, meanwhile, include spending and investment in the domestic economy from foreign sources, plus inflows of foreign aid.

pluses and minuses

While mercantilism—which held sway between the 16th and 18th centuries in Britain, mainland Europe, and North America—held that a trade surplus was vital to a country's economic health, modern economists have a far more nuanced approach. In bad economic times, it is preferable to run a surplus, since healthy exports means more domestic jobs and thus higher domestic demand that spurs economic growth. However, when the economy is booming, running a deficit floods the domestic market with sufficient goods and services to meet demand but also encourages price competition that keeps inflation in check. Nonetheless, if a government sees long-term unfavorable trends in the trade balance, it may be tempted to impose some form of protectionism to bring about a rebalance (see page 148).

fair trading?

In the years between the two world wars, the international trading system reached the point of collapse as countries riven by recession devalued their currencies to bring down the cost of their exports in the hope of growing their share of what was a shrinking global market. After World War II, many of the world's leading economies signed up to the Bretton Woods Agreement (see page 162). Among its provisions was the pegging of currencies to the U.S. dollar to avoid further unilateral devaluations and the establishment, in 1947, of a General Agreement on Tariffs and Trade (GATT). Such instruments were designed to introduce a new climate of cooperation between trading partners to avert further turmoil of the type seen in the interwar years. The Bretton Woods Agreement came to an end in 1971, when Richard Nixon depegged the dollar from gold in order to have greater freedom in determining money supply. Naturally, every country wants to negotiate the best terms of trade for itself, yet there remains a consensus that the interests of individual states and the world at large are best served by a cooperative and broadly fair international trading system.

what is the WTO for?

The World Trade Organization (WTO) grew out of and succeeded GATT in 1995 as the body responsible for policing global trade. It is there to ensure that international commerce "flows as smoothly, predictably, and freely as possible," a mission that allows for the adoption of certain protectionist measures. It has some 160 member nations, all of which are legally bound to uphold WTO laws. That means any business based in a member country must also abide by them. It is estimated that WTO rules govern over 97% of all trade. With headquarters in Geneva, Switzerland, it also serves as a mediator in disputes between member countries. If it fails to resolve a conflict through negotiation, it can impose penalties, such as trade sanctions, against the offending nation. Given its power, the WTO has its critics, who accuse it variously of lacking accountability, supporting undemocratic and brutal regimes as long as they espouse free trade, and acting against the interests of poorer nations. With regard to this last charge, for instance, the WTO's approach to intellectual-property protection has been attacked, with claims that large pharmaceutical companies' interests have been protected and developing nations priced out of the market for essential, but patented, drugs. The WTO has also been accused of doing too little to deter antidumping measures (see next page) by wealthy nations and of favoring developed nations intent on maintaining agricultural subsidies that effectively bar developing nations from the market.

comparative advantage

Along with Adam Smith, David Ricardo was the leading figure of early classical economics. His theory of comparative advantage is pivotal to understanding how international trade works.

Much of Ricardo's thinking on international trade was a response to mercantilism, which ultimately, he believed, led to inefficient use of resources and restricted wealth generation. For example, he opposed the imposition of the Corn Laws in 1815, which saw a ban on imports of wheat from Europe into Britain. As a result of that legislation, wheat prices rose in the UK, benefiting a minority of rich landowners who helped push the law through but not the great majority of the people who were unable to afford to feed themselves. Allowing the importation of wheat, Ricardo argued, would have been to the wider benefit of British society.

Adam Smith had already established that trade benefited both importing and exporting countries where one country has an absolute advantage in production—in other words, where one country can produce a product more efficiently than the other. For instance, imagine two countries: Vinland and Chipland. Vinland has the perfect climate for viticulture, while Chipland has ideal conditions for growing potatoes. In this scenario, it makes perfect sense for Vinland to focus on wine production and Chipland on potato cultivation, with each exporting their produce to the other.

comparatively speaking

Ricardo built on Smith's work to develop the theory of comparative advantage, which explains why trade can benefit countries even when one country has an absolute advantage in all products. Ricardo argued that it still makes sense for countries to specialize in certain goods and services and import what it does not specialize in. At the heart of comparative advantage is the idea of opportunity cost. Ricardo said it makes sense to specialize in what you're very best at, even if you're better at everything. Imagine Vinland again, but this time its potential trading partner is Secondbestland.

The populations of both countries want bread and wine. Vinland can produce not only wine far more efficiently but is also better placed to produce bread, too. For instance, it takes Vinland 50 hours of labor to produce 100 bottles of wine, and 60 hours of labor to produce 1000 loaves of bread. Secondbestland needs 80 hours of labor to produce 100 bottles of wine and 70 hours to produce 1000 loaves of bread. According to the theory of absolute advantage, Vinland ought to produce all the bread and wine. But if we look at the opportunity cost—the next-best opportunity forgone by making a particular choice— involved, we see that the labor Vinland directs toward bread production costs it 6/5 units of wine, while the equivalent opportunity cost in Secondbestland is 7/8 units of wine. Therefore, Vinland should specialize in wine production and Secondbestland in bread production.

In other words, it takes Vinland a combined 110 hours of labor to produce 100 bottles of wine and 1000 loaves of bread. It takes Secondbestland 150 hours to produce the same. Their combined 260 hours of labor produces 200 bottles of wine and 2000 loaves. But if the countries specialize, Vinland can produce 220 bottles of wine in 110 hours, and Secondbestland can produce 2143 loaves in 150 hours. Therefore, aggregate production has increased with no additional labor inputs. Ricardo thus showed how international trade works in everyone's best interests even where one country has absolute advantage in all industries.

David Ricardo

Ricardo was born to Dutch-Jewish émigré parents in London in 1772, and when he was 14 he began working for his father as a stockbroker. However, aged 21, the two fell out over religion, with Ricardo Jr. becoming a Christian and marrying a Quaker girl, Priscilla Wilkinson. Setting up in business on his own, he earned a fortune dealing in government securities.

He became interested in economics as an academic discipline after reading Adam Smith's *Wealth of Nations* in 1799. Ricardo published his first economic treatise, *The High Price of Bullion* in 1810 and associated with some of the leading economists of the day, including Malthus, James Mill, and Jeremy Bentham. In 1814, Ricardo authored the influential *Essay on the Influence of a Low Price of Corn*. His landmark *Principles of Political Economy and Taxation* followed in 1817. He retired as a broker in 1819 and subsequently became a member of parliament. He died in in Gloucestershire in 1823 from an ear infection, leaving an estate worth around £100 million at today's prices. His systematic approach to economic thinking and his innovative theories on subjects including the labor theory of value, diminishing returns, wages, rent, and money supply helped define classical economics. However, his championing of laissez-faire trade, an argument he rooted in empirical evidence, is probably his best and enduring contribution to the field. He and Smith stand as perhaps the two greatest figures of pre-20th-century economics.

a protective arm

While governments naturally want to protect their own, actions that excessively skew international trade are in no one's long-term interest.

"Protectionism" refers to the various actions and policies of a government to restrict international trade in order to protect local business interests from foreign competition:

- Tariffs—taxes levied on imported goods. It is common for governments to tax imports, but by ramping up the rates for specific goods, a government may hope to make it more cost-effective to buy local.
- Subsidies—monies from government given to businesses to make them more competitive against foreign competitors.
- Import quotas—a legally binding limit restriction on the volume of certain goods that may be imported. By limiting import volumes, importers are less able to exploit economies of scale, making imports more costly for consumers, hence less desirable.
- Export subsidies—monies paid by a government directly to exporters to encourage increased levels of exports.
- Red tape—a government may impose requirements, such as certification of safety standards or environmental standards, that serve as barriers to imports.
- Antidumping laws—legislation designed to stop foreign companies from flooding a domestic market with goods deemed to be unfairly cheap, perhaps because they have been manufactured using cheap labor.
- Exchange-rate manipulation—government intervention in foreign-exchange markets to artificially lower the value of its currency in order to raise the cost of imports/lower the cost of exports.
- Patents—it has been argued that some nations use patent law as a means to exclude competitors from the market.
- Advertising campaigns—governments exhort citizens to buy domestic goods.

setting trade free

For advocates of free trade, protectionism has a negative impact even on those it should benefit. For instance, consumers have to buy higher-priced domestic goods not cheaper foreign ones, while companies have less incentive to innovate in order to be competitive. Furthermore, to protect uncompetitive sectors, capital is diverted away from those industries in which a country has natural comparative advantage.

what is a trade war?

Tit-for-tat protectionist actions by rival nations can lead to a trade war. This can see a crisis in one particular trading sector spill over into other areas of the economy, and indeed draw in other countries not involved in the initial dispute. While it has not yet descended into a fully fledged trade war, the increasing antagonism between the world's two biggest economies—the U.S. and China—over alleged protectionist policies has caused international concern. Washington has repeatedly questioned the trading methods that have underpinned China's remarkable economic rise in the last 20 years or so. It has accused the Chinese government of illegally subsidizing some industrial sectors and of introducing cyber-security legislation that effectively regulates Western companies out of particular markets. Furthermore, the U.S. government has consistently accused Beijing of currency manipulation against the dollar in order to bring down the price of Chinese exports and raise the cost of its imports, allegations China has always refuted. Meanwhile, China accuses the U.S. of implementing its own protectionist practices, notably via unfair antidumping measures. With trade between the two nations exceeding $500 billion per year, it is in the interests of the global trading system that relations between two of its principal players do not sour too much.

coming to blows

Protectionism has historically been a source of international tensions, even prompting wars, including the American War of Independence against the British. Indeed, in 2009, the G20—a grouping of finance ministers from 19 of the world's largest national economies plus the EU—pledged: "We will not repeat the historic mistakes of protectionism of previous eras."

149

one big family

With each passing year, the world's economy becomes evermore integrated—a manifestation of the prevailing trend toward globalization. But is it all good news in our rapidly expanding global village?

In economic terms, globalization describes the process by which businesses and other organizations expand their influence from domestic to international settings. In practical terms, it explains why you can buy an identical Big Mac or iPhone or a pair of Nike sneakers in London, New York, and Addis Ababa.

Globalization arguably began in earnest with the opening up of international trade routes by the Voyages of Discovery of the 15th and 16th centuries. However, the pace of globalization has accelerated in recent decades as technological innovation has allowed the expansion of transnational trade, communication, and migration.

The ultimate symbol of globalization is the multinational corporation that typically operates in markets around the world, trading in multiple currencies and harnessing a workforce picked from across the globe. Some multinationals boast annual revenues that outstrip the GDPs (gross domestic products) of entire countries. According to *Forbes*, for instance, Walmart is the world's largest company by revenue, operating over 10,000 stores in almost 30 countries and employing over two million people, which makes it the largest private employer in the world.

good for business and society?

Clearly, globalization is good for the balance sheets of such companies. Businesses have the ability to source the best staff and capital resources, access new markets and so spread their risk, and exploit economies of scale, the cost benefits that come with increased production. Meanwhile, the consumer is presented with a hitherto unimaginably large range of goods and services at affordable prices. Supporters of globalization point out that multinationals create jobs wherever they set up business, further boosting local economies through tax revenues and spreading entrepreneurial and technological expertise. In addition, globalization may be seen to break down social and cultural barriers, while increasing pressure on governments to adhere to internationally acceptable standards of conduct.

winners and losers

However, many analysts are far more circumspect about the benefits on offer, especially for the developing world. The entry of a large, international firm into a local market often spells doom for low-level domestic business interests that are unable to compete. Furthermore, if an international company pays above the local wage rate, it can lead to significant imbalances in the domestic economy. Meanwhile, the labor force in the firm's native territory may see jobs it would otherwise have had being shifted overseas. Companies may be accused of wielding undue influence over governments of developing countries keen to attract their business. For some analysts, globalization has gone hand in hand with accelerated environmental and resource degradation, particularly in parts of the developing world where governments have prioritized economic development at almost any cost. For instance, some multinationals have been able to secure access to scarce water supplies for use in industrial processes at the expense of local populations' rights to clean water for drinking and sanitation.

do trading blocs add to or diminish globalization?

A trading bloc consists of a group of countries that encourage trade among themselves, while normally limiting imports from non-members. They are nothing new: the 13th-century Hanseatic League was an alliance of north European cities. However, the creation of transnational trading blocs has accelerated in the last 60 years, so that by the end of the 20th century over half of all business was conducted within them. Blocs may be established by countries within a clear geographical area (such as the EU) or through standalone agreements (such as the North American Free Trade Agreement). All trade blocs agree to reduce barriers of trade with each other by means of, for example, a preferential or free-trade agreement or the creation of a customs union, while a common market implies even closer economic integration, as in the EU.

So how do these often huge entities (the economies of the EU constitute by far the world's single largest economy) fit into the global scheme of things? They are vital components in the internationalization of trade, bringing millions of people into some degree of economic union. Yet, in a sense they are the antithesis of globalization, fracturing and distorting the global trading system, restricting non-member competitor states from entry into markets while bloc members may miss out on the potential benefits of trading with non-member nations.

dependency theory

Hans Singer and Raúl Prebisch provided the insights that formed the basis of dependency theory, which argues that international trade enriches wealthy nations at the expense of poorer ones.

Singer and Prebisch were credited with the creation of the Prebisch–Singer thesis even though they never worked together. Independently (and near contemporaneously) they drew similar conclusions about the nature of international trade. Singer published his paper in 1949, but Prebisch, who published a year later, received considerably more attention.

Both believed that international trade patterns are instrumental in evolving a divide between rich "core" nations and poor "peripheral" ones. This went against the widely made argument, rooted in the economics of David Ricardo, that international trade benefits everyone. The problem, as Singer and Prebisch saw it, can be traced to the differing nature of exports provided by developing and developed nations. Developing countries tend to export more raw materials, the demand for which changes only slowly, that developed countries buy and turn into manufactured, value-added goods, the demand for which grows more rapidly.

for richer, for poorer

What does the differing nature of these export groups mean for the developing nations, according to the Prebisch–Singer thesis? In short, developing countries tended to have worse terms of trade. That is, for nations that principally exported commodities and raw materials prices of exports remain fairly stable or reduce as productivity increases, while export prices of manufactured goods increase in response to growing demand, even as productivity gains are made by technological advances in the developed economy. The net result is that developing countries can buy fewer imports proportionate to the amount of exports they produce. This, dependency theorists contend, ensures that developing nations are consistently deprived of a strong bargaining position and are thus forced to accept ever less favorable trading terms that lock them into a cycle of poverty and dependency on wealthier trading partners.

Prebisch believed that developing nations ought to consider imposing protectionist policies, such as tariffs on imports, in order to reduce reliance on imports from abroad. He argued that many developing countries would be better served by looking to grow their economies by means other than export earnings. Specifically, he advocated the adoption of import substitution industrialization (ISI)—which means growing domestic production so as to be able to reduce dependency on foreign nations.

exploiting opportunities

The work of Singer and Prebisch was built upon by economists—including Andre Gunder Frank, Paul Baran, and Celso Furtado—under the broad banner of dependency theory, which reached its zenith in the 1960s and 1970s. As dependency theory evolved, it expanded to look not only at patterns of import and export but issues such as how foreign investment can lead to labor and resource exploitation in poorer countries. Critics of dependency theory, meanwhile, have pointed to the likes of South Korea and, more recently, China to show how international trade can fuel development as well as the failures of assorted nations that have adopted the isolationist policies implied by Prebisch. Nonetheless, dependency theory remains an alluring thesis to those skeptical that the rise of globalization will help address issues of global wealth inequality.

Raúl Prebisch

Born in 1901 in San Miguel de Tucumán in Argentina Raúl Prebisch began studying economics at the University of Buenos Aires in 1918, joining its economics faculty after graduating. From 1925 until 1948 he served as its professor of political economy. Alongside his academic posting, in the 1920s he also served in senior positions in the national department of statistics and the national bank. From 1930–2 he was Argentina's undersecretary of finance, and from 1935–48 he was director general of its central bank. He was then appointed executive secretary of the United Nations Economic Commission for Latin America (ECLA), where he stayed until 1963, carrying out much of his life's most important work.

In 1950 his seminal "The Economic Development of Latin America and Its Principal Problems" was published, which had, in part, been inspired by Singer's own related paper of the previous year. Prebisch's ideas on how best to progress economic development—including increased state intervention—were widely backed in Argentina and South America as a whole over the following couple of decades, earning Prebisch the somewhat inaccurate nickname of "the South American Keynes." From 1969, he served as director-general of the United Nations Latin American Institute for Economic and Social Planning. He died of a heart attack while in Santiago, Chile, in 1986.

under the counter

A vast swathe of economic activity goes unregulated and unmonitored. This is the Wild West of economics.

The informal economy goes by a number of names: the underground, shadow, or hidden economy, and the black market. It is defined by the World Bank as including all market-based legal economic activities that are left undisclosed to the relevant authorities, normally to short-circuit government-imposed rationing or price controls, to avoid paying taxes or having to fulfill other legal obligations (say, minimum wages or working conditions), or to bypass red tape. Some economists include illegal economic activities, such as smuggling and prostitution, in the definition.

Entities in the informal economy range from the lowliest sole trader to complex operations with large workforces. Typically, employees earn a below-average wage and receive none of the job protection available to those in the formal economy. The informal economy thrives where official institutions are absent or ineffective, where opportunities to join the formal economy are restricted, and where there is a demand for goods and services (usually at low cost) that formal businesses do not meet.

the great unseen

Attributing a precise value to a sector defined by lack of transparency is, inevitably, hard. Nonetheless, there are some startling statistics. The Organisation for Economic Co-operation and Development (OECD) reported in 2009 that around 1.8 billion people globally worked in the shadow economy. Worth in excess of $10 trillion per year, the sector's GDP outstrips that of every nation bar the U.S. and China. The World Bank reported, for the period 1997–2007, no fewer than 13 nations in which the informal economy made up more than 50% of the total economy, with Bolivia topping the list at 66.1%. The disparity between rich and poor countries is striking, too, with the high-income nations of the OECD having informal economies averaging between 10% and 15% of GDP, while across sub-Saharan Africa the figure is close to 40%. Clearly the informal economy plays a vital role in the world economic picture. If it were to be phased out overnight, we could safely predict the collapse of the global economy.

how does the internet facilitate illegal trade?

One of the most disturbing aspects of the internet boom has been the growth of the dark web. This is composed of darknets—encrypted cyber networks that operate "invisibly" to those without the relevant software and access permissions. The dark web has become a haven for criminal activity. It has facilitated trade in contraband, from child pornography to arms and drugs. Perhaps the most famous dark website of them all was Silk Road, a platform used for buying and selling narcotics. Named after the network of trade routes that linked Europe and Asia in centuries past, Silk Road began operating in 2011 under the stewardship of a figure known as Dread Pirate Roberts, who portrayed himself as a libertarian hero. Trade was carried out using the bitcoin cyber currency, which is notoriously difficult to track so further aiding Silk Road users in disguising their identities. Between February and July 2012, it was estimated that some $15 million of business was carried out on the site. However, in 2013, the FBI moved to close the site and arrested one Ross Ulbricht on suspicion of being Dread Pirate Roberts. He received a life sentence in May 2015.

order from chaos

While the informal economy is inherently lawless and unregulated, it supports innovative entrepreneurs who otherwise might be excluded altogether from profitable endeavor. As Robert Neuwirth, author of *Stealth of Nations: The Global Rise of the Informal Economy*, said: "What happens in all the unregistered markets and roadside kiosks of the world is not simply haphazard. It is a product of intelligence, resilience, self-organization, and group solidarity, and it follows a number of well-worn although unwritten rules. It is, in that sense, a system."

in development

We often hear the terms "developed" and "developing" worlds, but what do these labels actually mean, and who decides which countries qualify for which tag?

In crude terms, the developed world has traditionally encompassed the nations that we tend think of as rich—North America, Western Europe and Australasia, along with Japan—while developing world has served as a euphemism for most of the rest of the planet. The phrases have largely come to replace more antiquated and arguably politically weighted expressions such as "First World" and "Third World." However, there are no standard catch-all definitions. Instead, the terms have evolved their meanings and become more nuanced over time.

So, what criteria does the modern-day economist look to when considering the development status of a country or region?

- A developed region will have a sound economic footing with relatively high levels of total and per capita (the average per person) GDP. A developing region is likely to suffer from economic insecurity, with its citizens generally experiencing a lower standard of living.
- A developed economy is dominated by industrial and/or service sectors, whereas a developing economy tends to have a much higher proportion of agriculture.
  - A developed economy will normally have an evolved infrastructure, including sophisticated transport networks. A developing economy may well not.
  - A developed region will traditionally have well-established democratic institutions that provide a level of political security. Developing economies are often, although by no means always, characterized by political fragility.
- A developed economy is likely to score better in other measures of social advancement, such as literacy, educational attainment, and health—indicators encapsulated in the United Nations' Human Development Index, which rates countries on an aggregate score.

blurred lines

These are labels attributed on the basis of opinion. The WTO (see page 157), for example, allows members to choose their status, with preferential terms sometimes available to those who proclaim developing status. A country or region may alter its designation, most often from developing to developed, by common consent. While Japan, for instance, was once seen as Asia's sole developed nation, South Korea is now often included, too. China is a more troubling case. It is the world's second largest economy, yet it suffers huge levels of poverty, it has weak democratic credentials, and other social indicators also lag behind.

The UN, meanwhile, operates an additional classification of least developed country (LDC) on the basis of poverty (a country must fall below a set level of per capita income), low human development indicators (related to nutrition, health, education, and adult literacy), and economic vulnerability (such as weak agriculture, low exports, and propensity to natural disasters). As of 2014, there were 48 LDCs that qualified for special aid and support from a total of 193 states recognized by the UN.

what are the UN MDGs?

The UN's Millennium Development Goals (MDGs) are a program of eight goals, encompassing economics, health, the environment, and social justice, designed to improve conditions in the developing world. The entire membership of the UN

(189 countries at the time) adopted the package of targets in 2000, and several major international organizations also signed up. The goals, which had an original completion deadline of 2015, are to:

- eradicate extreme hunger and poverty;
- achieve universal primary education;
- promote gender equality and empower women;
- reduce child mortality;
- improve maternal health;
- combat HIV/AIDS, malaria, and other diseases;
- ensure environmental sustainability;
- and to develop a global partnership for development.

There have been notable successes, such as the cancelation in 2005 of some $50 billion in debt owed by members of the heavily indebted poor countries (HIPC). Critics, however, question the vagueness of some of the goals and the difficulties in measuring success. The UN, too, acknowledges that much remains to be done. In 2015, UN Secretary-General Ban Ki-moon reported:

> "The MDGs helped to lift more than a billion people out of extreme poverty, to make inroads against hunger, to enable more girls to attend school than ever before and to protect our planet… Yet for all the remarkable gains, I am keenly aware that inequalities persist and that progress has been uneven."

raising the bar

What is to be done to improve the economies of the developing world? That is the question that development economics attempts to answer.

Development economics studies how micro- and macroeconomic growth can be fostered in developing nations. It is a wide-ranging area that considers a nation's or region's political and social institutions alongside its particular economic conditions. Economic development commonly involves large-scale structural changes, such as instigating legal frameworks for market transactions and labor conditions, establishing democratic and accountable governments, and ensuring health, education, and welfare provision.

How to promote development can vary significantly from country to country. In 1943 the Austro-Hungarian-born Paul Rosenstein-Rodan outlined the big-push model that calls for a surge of synchronized investment across multiple business sectors. However, such a strategy relies on the cooperation of a non-corrupt central administration with a clear idea on which sectors are ripe for growth. Yet even a well-intentioned government may struggle to know which new industries will take off and which will not.

By the 1980s, there was a move toward taking development out of the hands of governments and trusting in the market to deliver. To this end, the Washington Consensus—essentially a package of free-market reforms—became the dominant development doctrine. Yet critics soon noted that the Consensus barely recognized the circumstances of individual countries nor the fact that many of the world's poorest countries are run by political elites with little interest in reducing their political and economic influence in favor of reform. So, something of a hybrid strategy has developed, called the market-friendly approach. It acknowledges the role of markets in bolstering developing economies as well as that of the state in correcting market failures, such as the problem of securing credit for new businesses.

how best to help

The nations of the developed world contribute to international development in a number of ways. Direct investment, for instance, not only introduces finance into the recipient country but also allows for the sharing of skills and experience as well as, in theory at least, consolidating a culture of doing business to internationally accepted standards. However, perhaps the most visible form of international development is international aid, whereby one country provides economic assistance to another. This can take several forms, including: direct aid, such as provision of food supplies; indirect aid—financing for infrastructure projects, for example; and debt relief (see page 139).

Well-administered aid doubtless provides a boon to the recipient country, allowing it to recover from short-term crises such as natural disasters as well as providing a framework for longer-term economic development. But critics of foreign aid argue that it imposes a culture of dependency on donor nations (which donor nations may be tempted to exploit); distorts markets (for instance, food aid can negatively impact on the revenues of local food producers); and is liable to be misdirected and misused where recipient governments lack transparency and accountability. Nonetheless, it remains a fundamental component of international development, with the United Nations recommending that rich nations contribute at least 0.7% of their GDP to foreign aid.

how do you solve a problem like sub-Sahara?

Sub-Saharan Africa is recognized as the world's poorest major region. Almost half the population live in poverty, and attempts at development have been stifled by war, endemic corruption, natural disaster, weak social, legal, and government institutions, and poor health and education provision—issues that have not been satisfactorily addressed in the postcolonial era.

However, the picture is slowly changing. In 2011, according to *The Economist,* six of the ten fastest-growing economies in the world were: Angola, Chad, Ethiopia, Mozambique, Nigeria, and Rwanda. Of course, a weak economy can grow faster than a strong one—so, if your GDP is $100 million, it is easier to add a further 10% ($10 million) than to add 10% to a GDP of $100 billion (an additional $10 billion)—but nonetheless, the statistic is striking. This economic expansion has been driven primarily by remittances from workers abroad plus high levels of direct foreign investment, much of it originating from the fast-growing BRICS nations (see page 111). In the 2010s, private capital inflows into sub-Saharan Africa outstripped foreign aid. Its vast mineral reserves have attracted foreign money, notably from the mineral-hungry, industry-driven economies of China and India. The future of the region is far from secure, but, should it make strides toward long-term political stability, its prospects look more rosy now than they have for many years.

entitlement theory

Rooted in analysis of the famine that ravaged Bengal in 1943, Amartya Sen established that famine is not principally the lack of food but the result of inequalities in food distribution.

Sen expounded his theory on the causes of famine in a 1981 paper entitled "Poverty and Famines: An Essay on Entitlement and Deprivation." It was a subject area in which he had direct experience, having been a nine-year-old growing up in Bengal in northwest India when famine struck in 1943, causing the death of some three million people. Sen came from a relatively affluent background, being the son of a university professor, and he, his family, and wider social circle went largely untouched by the disaster. In fact, it was only when a severely malnourished man arrived at his school that he became aware of the tragedy unfolding around him. That famine was significantly more likely to affect the poor than the wealthy affected him greatly.

When he came to write his paper, he used data from the Bengal famine and later famines in Africa and Asia to show that lack of food was not the principal driver of disaster. For example, in Bengal food production had declined year on year but was still higher than it had been in earlier, famine-free years. In other words, there should have been enough food to go around, so something else must have happened to deprive those who needed it most.

lack of entitlements

Sen established that it was landless, rural farmworkers and the urban poor who died in the greatest numbers. With India under British rule at the time, the government

in London had pumped money into the economy to bolster the Indian contribution to the war effort as World War II raged in Europe. Most of this money gravitated toward the region's major city, Kolkata. With more cash to spend in the Kolkatan economy, consumer demand increased, resulting in rising prices, including for staple foods. Against this backdrop, the rural population and the urban poor were unable to secure sufficient wages to keep up.

Sen termed the goods and services that an individual can access as entitlements. Kolkata, like any other market-based economy, oversaw a system in which most people accessed entitlements by exchanging them for money, which, in turn, was exchanged for labor. When incomes lost pace against prices, individuals became unable to access their entitlements—most crucially, food—despite there being food to be accessed. In many cases, then, famine may be regarded as entitlement failure rather than natural disaster. Sen's work has proved highly influential on governments and those international organizations battling food crises. Policy-makers now routinely seek to address famine not only by providing emergency food relief but by striving to ensure food-price stability and by seeking ways to maintain sufficient incomes for the poorest parts of society.

Amartya Sen

Amartya Sen was born in Santiniketan, West Bengal, in 1933. He obtained a degree in economics in Calcutta (now Kolkata) then won a scholarship to Trinity College, Cambridge, graduating with a second BA in economics in 1955. He then headed the Department of Economics at Jadavpur University, Kolkata, before returning to Cambridge to study philosophy. Subsequently he held a series of academic positions in Delhi, in the UK at the London School of Economics, and the universities of London and Oxford, and at a number of U.S. Ivy League colleges. From 1998 until 2004 he was master of Trinity College, Cambridge, before taking up the post of Thomas W. Lamont University Professor of Economics and Philosophy at Harvard. He received the Nobel Prize for Economics in 2008 for "contribution to welfare economics."

Sen's work, especially in the field of human capabilities, has had wide-ranging influence, including in the formulation of the Human Development Index published by the United Nations Development Program. Today, he is one of the leading figures in development economics and world-renowned for his work in social-choice theory, which looks at how choices are collectively made. Aside from his paper "Poverty and Famine," his other major works include *Collective Choice and Social Welfare* (1970), *Development and Freedom* (1999), and *The Idea of Justice* (2009).

big beasts

A number of supranational financial organizations transcend national borders to wield vast influence over the global economic landscape.

Such superbanks tend to be established by agreement between a group of countries to add economic stability to a region, facilitate cooperation between nations, and, in many cases, guarantee liquidity if a member state runs into financial problems. These include the African Development Bank, the Asian Development Bank, the European Central Bank, the European Bank for Reconstruction and Development and the Inter-American Development Bank. The two institutions with the farthest reach are the International Monetary Fund (IMF) and the International Bank for Reconstruction and Development (IBRD), commonly known as the World Bank. Both institutions came into being as a result of the 1944 Bretton Woods Agreement.

Bretton Woods

The Bretton Woods Agreement looked to reconfigure the global economic landscape in the aftermath of World War II. The World Bank's specific remit was to assist reconstruction in European and Asian countries that had suffered significant war damage. Over the ensuing decades, its mission evolved—today it provides financial aid and technical assistance to developing countries. Loans can be accessed only for state-run or state-guaranteed projects; loans to the private sector are offered by an affiliate organization, the International Finance Corporation.

The IMF was established to promote economic cooperation between nations and to bring stability to the global economy, reflecting a desire to restore equilibrium in the postwar period and recognition of the need to avoid a repeat of the traumatic economic upheavals that accompanied the depression of the 1930s.

Today, the IMF is principally concerned with establishing and maintaining rules governing the international monetary system that drives global trade, keeping a watchful eye on the state of member economies—virtually every country in the world—making loans to countries as they need them, and offering practical assistance and expert support where necessary. It is common that loans to countries in trouble come with demands that the recipient country undergo a reform program in accordance with IMF guidelines.

who polices the economic police?

Opponents of the IMF most commonly criticize it for promoting the liberal free-market economic agenda favored by the developed world without giving due consideration to other economic models. In particular, critics cite the conditions it imposes when issuing loans, arguing that the organization too often demands reforms at the expense of wider social welfare. Renowned economist Joseph Stiglitz went so far as to say that in its attachment to monetarism the IMF "was not participating in a conspiracy, but it was reflecting the interests and ideology of the Western financial community." For instance, it has been convincingly argued that the austerity measures imposed on Argentina in the early 21st century following its debt crisis led to a decline in public spending with long-term negative repercussions. Meanwhile, exponents of the pure free market criticize the IMF for being too interventionist and not allowing the markets to establish their own natural balance. Others suggest that, as the organization at the top of the financial tree, the IMF lacks accountability and is overly keen to flex its considerable political muscle. Its defenders, however, point to the fact that acceptance of its authority—and, by extension, acceptance of its loans and their attached conditions—is purely voluntary on the part of nation states. For more than 70 years the IMF has had the impossible task of keeping all parties happy—but then no one said that bossing the global economy would be easy.

what happens when economics & politics collide?

what went wrong?

Keynesianism

we, the people

the people problem

the silver bullet

war: what is it good for?

economics & the environment

economics & religion

women count

what went wrong?

The global economic slowdown that began in the 21st century was arguably the defining economic event of our lifetimes, in no small part because it was not widely foreseen. So just why did the world's economy go into reverse?

The crisis began when the U.S. property bubble burst in 2007. With the world's biggest national economy caught on the hop, economic uncertainty spread quickly. As country after country lurched into recession (experienced two or more quarters of economic contraction) trillions of dollars were wiped off the markets, millions found themselves without a job, consumer spending was strangled, and debt default rife. Indeed, the entire period 2008–13 has become known as the "Great Recession."

Since 2007, analysts have struggled to understand quite why it all went so wrong so quickly, shattering developed-world economies that had enjoyed hitherto unprecedentedly long periods of prosperity. Most economists agree that a number of factors came into play and that we were caught in the eye of a perfect storm.

countdown to disaster

First came the so-called credit crunch, whereby credit availability slumped and came with more stringent conditions attached. For years, the relative economic stability of the developed world had nurtured a culture of easy credit. However, by 2007 it was evident that house prices in many countries—starting with the U.S.—had risen excessively quickly, driven by the ready availability of mortgages. When the housing bubble burst, many people found themselves unable to make repayments on properties now often worth less than the mortgages taken out on them. Meanwhile, banks were left with swathes of bad debt that was unlikely ever to be repaid.

Worse, many of these bad debts had been packaged into complex financial bundles (often with good debt) and sold between financial institutions and investors, many of whom did not fully understand the intricacies of the debt bundles. It has been argued that such derivatives were made possible thanks to a climate of deregulation that lapsed into under-regulation. Whatever the reason, banks throughout Europe were now exposed to the difficulties in the U.S. housing market.

Soon, many banks found themselves in serious financial straits, unable to raise credit to ensure liquidity. Investor and consumer confidence was affected, leading to reduced consumer spending and even runs on some banks. Furthermore, the slowdown in credit and consumer spending prompted a contraction in world trade. Meanwhile, the problems in the U.S. and Europe were intensified because oil prices continued to rise thanks to ongoing demand from the emerging economies of China and India.

Such was the negative impact of the Lehman Brothers bankruptcy (see page 103) that from 2008 most governments agreed to step in to save other major financial institutions on the brink of bankruptcy—a strategy that preserved a degree of confidence in the markets but which came at a heavy cost to national treasuries. Faced with severely weakened financial sectors, reduced trade, rising unemployment, and national debt plus low consumer spending, the economies of the U.S. and Europe were ravaged by recession.

calming the storm: QE

Governments undertook an array of initiatives in a bid to counter the effects of the slowdown and foster growth. In doing so, the term "quantitative easing" entered the public lexicon. But what does it mean?

It has been noted that the Great Recession represented the biggest, most widespread economic shock since World War II and the Great Depression that preceded it. Among

what prompted the eurozone crisis?

While the U.S. took a battering in the Great Recession, Europe—and specifically the nations of the eurozone—arguably suffered the greater consequences. Many European states suffered double-dip recessions, coming out of an initial recession only to soon lapse into another. The crisis highlighted the high national debt burdens carried by several nations, including Spain, Portugal, Ireland, and, most notoriously, Greece. Additional problems included property bubbles, low tax revenues—a particular problem for some southern European states—and faltering exports. With eurozone bonds losing value and central banks unable or unwilling to prop them up, many European governments were forced to introduce austerity measures—huge cuts in state spending to reduce government costs that also constrict economic activity, prompting increased unemployment and social discontent—in return for financial bailouts.

For the eurozone, this raised fundamental questions. Is it possible to integrate a large group of countries with vastly different economic profiles? Is it fair that the richer members support those that have got into trouble? If so, should those wealthier neighbors be permitted to enforce stringent conditions on a bailout? Would it be better for everyone to cut their losses and set Greece loose? Such questions may yet decide the entire future of the European Union.

the somewhat limited arsenal of weapons that governments could call upon to try to turn the economic tide were interest-rate cuts and fiscal-stimulus programs. By cutting interest rates to historically low levels, it was hoped credit would become more easily available, prompting broader economic activity. However, a cowed banking sector short of funds remained reluctant to encourage borrowing and was slow to pass on interest-rate cuts to customers. Fiscal stimuli, however, were arguably more successful, as governments offered targeted tax cuts and undertook spending programs with the aim of kick-starting the economy.

However, it was the relatively new strategy of quantitative easing (QE) that garnered much of the attention, with economists sharply divided as to its efficacy. Quantitative easing involves a central bank creating money which it then uses to buy bonds. The money it uses thus flows into financial institutions, theoretically increasing liquidity in the financial sector, which, in turn, should prompt lending and so increase economic activity. It is a bit like a defibrillator for an ailing economy, employed when interest rates cannot be reasonably lowered any further.

success or failure?

QE was initially put into operation in the early 2000s in Japan, which was then emerging from its own lost decade after a major economic collapse in the early 1990s. During the Great Recession, QE was employed by the U.S. Federal Reserve, the Bank of England, and throughout the eurozone, where it was known as Long-Term Refinancing Operations. Since QE was undertaken through transactions with major institutions, there was no need to print wheelbarrow-loads of new cash. Instead new money was "magicked" out of thin air and added to electronic balance sheets. The cost of this financial sleight of hand has run into trillions of dollars.

So did it work? The jury is very much out. Overall, there is evidence that QE did increase liquidity, so that new money eventually found its way into the economy. However, it took several waves of QE before there was any discernible impact, making it a very expensive course of action as far as taxpayers are concerned. The problem was that financial institutions, concerned with their own state of health, could not resist the temptation to stockpile the money pumped in rather than freeing it up for the individuals and businesses for whom it was really intended. Only as economic conditions improved and under intense government pressure did the banks pass on their windfall. In the long term, the creation of all that new money will inevitably push prices up, especially when coupled with low interest rates, but many governments felt they had no choice but to unleash QE, with inflation regarded amid the general economic turmoil as a bridge to be crossed much further down the line.

how does money grow?

While, as we have seen, flooding the economy with new money is not without its problems, advocates of QE argue that the multiplier effect ensures the positives outweigh the negatives. Rooted in the 1930s theories of John Maynard Keynes—whose work enjoyed a renaissance as the global slowdown took hold in the 2000s—the multiplier effect occurs because of the way banks lend money. The effect is that, for every unit of currency created by the central bank, an increased volume of currency enters the economy. So how does this apparently magical transformation come about? Because a capital sum can be lent and borrowed multiple times. Exactly how much a central bank's money breeds is dependent on the reserve rate, the amount banks keep back in order to pay depositors on demand. Imagine, for instance, that the reserve rate stands at 10%. So the U.S. Fed creates $100 which it deposits with the Bank of Boom. The Bank of Boom keeps $10 in reserve but loans $90 to a customer. That customer puts the money in the Friendly Bank, which retains $9 (10%) and loans out $81 to another customer. That customer deposits the money in the Bonanza Bank, which retains $8.10 (10%) but loans $72.90… and so on. Already the initial $100 has tripled in value, and so the cycle goes on. To calculate the maximum value of new money supply—assuming all the money is redeposited, which does not occur in real life—divide the initial sum by the reserve rate. In our case, our $100 is divided by 0.1 (or 10%), giving a maximum multiplier figure of $1000.

Keynesianism

One of the defining economic philosophies of the 20th century, Keynesianism argued that interventions to boost aggregate spending in the economy can spark recovery at times of economic crisis.

Before John Maynard Keynes appeared on the economic scene, the prevailing orthodoxy among classical and neoclassical economists was that cyclical declines in levels of employment and total economic output were of sufficiently small magnitude that the mechanisms of the market would bring about a self-correction. So, according to the classical model, if total demand falls with resulting lower production and rising unemployment, the laws of supply and demand will precipitate a drop in wages and prices. In a climate of low inflation and low wages, businesses will be tempted to make capital investments and employ more people, reigniting demand and restoring growth. However, the grim reality of the Great Depression—prompted by the Wall Street Crash of 1929—ushered in an unprecedented period of mass unemployment and poverty that spread across continents. Many hold that it also helped create the climate of political unrest in which Hitler and his fascist contemporaries were able to prosper. As the economic depression lingered, bringing misery to millions, Keynes became convinced that it was not enough to leave the markets to try to put things right.

the duty of government

Keynes's most influential work, *The General Theory of Employment, Interest, and Money*, appeared in 1936. In it he laid out his thesis that lower wages alone were not enough to bring about increased employment, since businesses were reluctant to bolster their workforces to produce goods for which there was little demand. By the same token, he argued, it was a myth that firms took advantage of low prices to make capital investments. Instead, he said, economic slumps rendered companies as reluctant to spend as consumers, reinforcing the cycle of low demand and rising unemployment.

Keynes's solution was for the government to step in and bolster demand by spending on public works, such as large transport-infrastructure projects. The state can thus provide economic stimulus in conditions where private enterprise is reluctant to do so. Or, bluntly put, a government can spend its way out of recession. For Keynes and his followers such expenditure represents a surer way to reignite the economy than any of the other options commonly available—such as attempting to manipulate money supply. His credo was warmly received by many governments at the eye of the Great Depression, and his theories were instrumental in the development of welfare states in many European countries in the aftermath of World War II.

However, by the 1970s, Keynesianism was losing its popularity, not least because it seemed impotent in the face of emerging stagflation. Much of the developed world instead turned toward monetarist policies (see page 124), although the market failures of the late 2000s prompted a reevaluation of Keynes's ideas.

John Maynard Keynes

John Maynard Keynes was born in 1883 in Cambridge, England, into an affluent family of academics. He was schooled at Eton before studying mathematics at King's College, Cambridge, where he graduated with a First. He then joined the civil service, working in the India Office, but returned to academic life in Cambridge in 1908. He was elected a fellow at King's in 1911, and his first book, *Indian Currency and Finance*, was published in 1913. During World War I he was employed by the Treasury and attended the Paris Peace Conference. Shortly afterward he published *The Economic Consequences of the Peace*, a coruscating and prophetic critique of the Treaty of Versailles that established him on the global academic stage. In the 1920s, he played the markets with significant success, while also serving as bursar of King's College and consolidating his reputation as a major macroeconomic thinker. In 1926, he married a Russian ballerina named Lydia Lopokova. In 1930, he published *A Treatise on Money*, and his reputation was secured with *The General Theory of Employment, Interest, and Money* six years later. He worked in the Bank of England during World War II, and in 1942 was awarded a peerage. Two years later he led Britain's delegation at the Bretton Woods Conference that created the IMF and World Bank. He died in East Sussex, England, in 1946. *The Economist* described him as "Britain's most famous 20th-century economist."

we, the people

One of the great economic challenges a government faces is keeping track of the changing nature of its population, which impacts not only what the population needs but what it can produce.

Demographics is the study of population, using indicators such as age, race, gender, and employment and educational status. Businesses look at demographics for a better understanding of the composition of the marketplace—by analyzing the characteristics of consumer groups, companies can better target their offerings. Demographics also inform economic policy. For instance, a government in a country with a rapidly aging population might increase investment in healthcare. In contrast, if the average age of the population is falling, a government may divert resources toward education.

The largest demographic challenge we face today is the steep rise in the world population. While it took until 1800 for world population to reach a billion, it now increases by a billion every 15 years or so. This means that there is vastly more demand for finite resources. In fact, the world has coped better with its population explosion than Thomas Malthus predicted some 200 years ago (see page 174), through more efficient use of resources thanks to technological advances.

more people, living longer

The key reasons for the population boom are decreasing levels of child mortality and longer lifespans. An increase in numbers of the very young and the old presents a problem of its own, since neither group is economically productive. In the long term, decreasing mortality enhances the size of the working population, but, in the interim, those children need looking after. The elderly, meanwhile, absorb a disproportionate amount of healthcare and need pensions, a ticking time-bomb considered on page 177.

Certain changes in the economy can prompt demographic changes that feed back into the economy. Technological advances, for example, have seen per-worker productivity reach new heights, leading to a decline in the number of workers required in many sectors. This has resulted in the proportion of working-age people outside the labor market increasing in many developed nations since the 1970s.

how have women changed the economic landscape?

Over the last hundred years the role of women has changed significantly. Whereas women were once tasked with being homemakers and childraisers, with perhaps a little cottage-industry work, they now make vital contributions in all areas, especially in the developed world. The demographic change in workforce composition was in no small part down to the success of the women's rights movements in Europe and North America in the early 20th century, allied to the demands for new sources of labor during the two world wars. Few serious economists argue that the expansion of the female workforce has been anything less than a triumph. According to OECD research, increases in female workforce participation—or a reduction in the gap between male and female participation—typically prompts a period of economic growth. However, serious gender inequalities hold the global economy back. In much of the developing world, formal employment for women—and better acccess to educational opportunities—on a mass scale remains a distant dream. In global terms, in 2013, the male employment-to-population ratio hovered around 72%, while the ratio for women was just over 47%, and women's average wages stood at around 60–75% of those of men. Such discrepancies need to be equalized if the global economy is to fully benefit from what women workers offer.

money and class

In another example of how the chicken-and-egg story of demographics and economics plays out, China has based its remarkable recent growth on labor-intensive, low-skilled industry. As the economy has boomed, workers have become richer, leading to the growth of the educated middle class. The country is likely to face a challenge in years to come to incorporate this influential section of the population into the economy, with a probable transition away from low-skilled, low-wage jobs to higher-skilled, high-wage roles.

the people problem

Writing in an age optimistic that society was set on a progressive course, Thomas Malthus offered a dissenting voice. He saw society locked into a cycle of long-term economic stagnation that would keep population expansion in check.

Malthus famously addressed what was to become known as the Malthusian Problem in his 1798 work, *An Essay on the Principle of Population*. Key to his argument was the belief that population grows broadly geometrically, while food production grows at an arithmetic rate. The latter situation, according to Malthus, was because of the law of diminishing returns: there is only so much land that can be used for food production, and the addition of more and more labor adds increasingly less output. The net result, he argued, is that population routinely grows at a pace that outstrips

expansion of the food supply so that food shortages become inevitable. In his words:

"The power of population is indefinitely greater than the power in the earth to produce subsistence for man."

However, he continued, balance is restored because malnutrition leads to an increased death rate, while the birth rate also declines as families decided to have fewer children since they do not have access to the food to support them. By this system of natural wastage, food resources come under less pressure, there is more to go around, and living conditions improve. Yet this benign situation is short-lived, since better living conditions bring about a reduction in the death rate and an increase in the birth rate, raising the population threshold again and lowering living standards until the population size goes back into decline. Thus we have the rather depressing Malthusian trap, in which the population is kept at a broadly constant level that the land can support over the long term. Furthermore, that population is bound into a cycle of economic stagnation, living on just enough and waiting for the next wave of starvation, disease, or other calamity to strike that will keep the population size in check.

the problem with no solution?

For Malthus, these were problems that could not be overcome either by the market or government intervention, social welfare serving only to encourage an increase in the birth rate, so compounding the problem. However, in the 200-plus years since Malthus's work, we have seen a population explosion and increasing living standards that prove he was not entirely on the right track. Crucially, he gave no consideration to the technological developments that have allowed us to produce more food despite the constraints of limited land.

While history has shown that Malthus was unduly pessimistic in his outlook, his theory nevertheless exerted significant influence as a counterforce to the optimism of many of his contemporaries in the fields of economics and political theory. While the consensus then was that society was set fair if it made the right calls on economic and social policies, Malthus suggested that the future was more significantly impacted by ineluctable natural laws. It was a divisive argument, strongly rejected, for instance, by Marx but proving influential on figures as disparate as Keynes and even Darwin. Today, his beliefs are echoed in the fears of those who believe our current rate of population expansion is unsustainable given the limited resource capacity of our planet.

Thomas Malthus

Thomas Malthus was born in 1766 in Surrey, England, into a well-to-do, liberal-leaning family. His interest in philosophy was fostered by two of his father's close friends, Jean-Jacques Rousseau and David Hume. He studied at Jesus College, Cambridge, from 1784; five years later he took religious orders, becoming a Church of England curate at a parish in Surrey.

In 1798, he published his landmark study on population growth, which underwent several revisions over the course of his lifetime. Around the end of the century, he spent a significant amount of time in Europe. In 1803, he became rector of Walesby in Lincolnshire, and the following year he married Harriet Eckersall. In 1805, he was named Professor of Political Economy at the East India Company College in Hertfordshire, and, in 1818, he was made a fellow of the Royal Society. In the 1820s, he took part in an intellectual tug-o'-war over fundamental questions of political economy with another great figure of the age, David Ricardo (see pages 146–7).

However, by the end of the decade, Malthus was an increasingly isolated figure, as the coming generation of economists eschewed many of his ideas. His other major works include *The Nature of Rent* (1815) and *Principles of Political Economy* (1820). He died in 1834.

the silver bullet

Perhaps the greatest single fiscal challenge to face governments of the developed world in decades to come will be how to pay for pensions as more people live longer.

Across the developed world, the elderly make up some 15% of the population. By 2030, that figure will be approaching 25%, and, by 2050, it will be 30%. In a few countries, including Japan, it is set to be closer to 35%. That is bad news for governments, with conservative estimates suggesting that public spending on pensions is set to rise from an average 11% of GDP to 18% over the next half century. There is simply not enough money in existing pension schemes to begin to cover these future obligations. For example, it was estimated that the U.S. pension program was underfunded by a trillion dollars back in 2008—not the sort of sum you can hope to find down the back of the couch.

how the pension crisis happened

How has the problem come about? In short, demographics. In the past, pensions for the elderly were supported by the productivity of the working-age population. But as people live to greater ages, there are no longer enough economically active citizens to prop up the system. In 1950, across the countries of the OECD, there were 7.2 people of working age (20–64) for every person over 65. In 2010, the ratio had fallen to 4.1:1. By 2050, it is predicted to be 2.1:1.

So what can be done? Most economists agree serious intervention is required. Three broad strategies are available, with many governments looking to deploy all three:

- **Revenue raising—governments can raise taxes and increase pension contributions to swell the pension-fund coffers.**
- **Remodeling—moving pensions from the defined-benefit model to the defined-contribution model (see page 98 for definitions), while also putting a cap on entitlements.**
- **Social engineering—redefining the worker-to-pensioner ratio by adapting employment law, increasing immigration for workers from abroad, and raising the retirement age (see the panel opposite).**

Many governments are also adopting a long-term strategy of encouraging the working-age population to make increased private provision for their senior years.

when are you clocking-off?

The old-age pension qualifying age varies from country to country. As of 2014, the average standard retirement age across OECD nations for males was 65 years, and for females 63.5. However, a large number of these countries have introduced programs of incremental rises that will see retirement ages increase over a period of several years. Some analysts suggest that a standard retirement age of 70 would be a fair reflection of increased life expectation. But raising the retirement age is, needless to say, a controversial measure. Its advocates argue that, however painful, it is a logical step. People stay healthy for longer, so why pension them off ahead of time when we can't afford to? Furthermore, by extending an individual's working life, you provide the government with increased tax revenues, which can be used toward provision of a higher basic pension, while giving the worker more opportunity to increase their personal wealth. Indeed, it is sometimes argued that a fixed retirement age is unfair to those who want to continue working into old age and also deprives the workforce of an invaluable pool of experience and expertise. However, critics point to the difficulties older people face in securing employment, particularly in manual labor. Furthermore, in countries where there is not full employment, the retention of older workers typically reduces employment opportunities for the young. Finally, there is the argument that raising the pensionable age is socially unjust, since it is the poorest who have to work longest, while the rich have the option to take early retirement and live off their private funds. The pensions crisis has no easy answer, but it is a problem that no government can afford to ignore.

war: what is it good for?

It is hard to manage an economy under relatively stable circumstances, let alone during a war. Nevertheless, war is a reality that actively molds the global economic landscape.

There is some truth in stating that war, while a human tragedy, can have positive repercussions for an economy. In wartime, governments have little choice but to increase their spending, which, in turn, leads to increased employment and an accompanying economic surge. There are also financial winners: conflict tends to be good news for arms traders and private military contractors, but it may also provide a fillip to a company that makes parachutes, military-grade boots, or freeze-dried food. Furthermore, when war means shortages and rationing, there is opportunity for aspiring black-marketeers.

However, these are temporary boosts to a tiny number of economic players. Rarely is war anything other than bad news for the economy as a whole. As Nobel Prize-winner Joseph Stiglitz said before the second Iraq War, conflict is "unambiguously bad in terms of what really counts: ordinary people's standard of living."

the costs of war

Here are a few of the ways in which war impacts economies:

- **Debt—wars are expensive, both in direct costs—additional military hardware, for example—and indirect costs, such as long-term care for wounded soldiers. War spending is typically met by loans, adding to the national debt burden.**
- **Higher taxes—as well as accruing loans, governments commonly increase taxes to pay for wars.**
- **Inflation—the influx of "new" money into the economy from increased government spending typically leads to price rises.**
- **Market instability—war makes investors nervous. As Stiglitz noted: "Markets loathe uncertainty and volatility. War, and anticipation of war, bring both."**

In addition, the potential growth of black markets can distort regular markets.

- Opportunity cost—that is, everything that would have been financed if resources were not diverted. The withdrawal of funding from, say, large-scale capital infrastructure projects can have serious repercussions on economic growth for years and even decades after the war that caused it has ended.
- Manpower loss—war kills and disables individuals who might otherwise have been economically productive.
- Long-term welfare costs—governments incur the cost of providing care and support to veterans and pensions to dependants of those killed in action.
- Distortions in international trade— conflict mitigates the free market. Not only does it become physically more difficult to transport goods but governments commonly impose sanctions and other restrictions on trade.
- Reconstruction costs—governments are required to rebuild what was destroyed.

In a best-case scenario, the end of conflict can restore political and social stability. In the case of Western Europe after World War II, it also fostered a period of infrastructural reconstruction and economic remodeling that led to an unprecedented period of affluence. However, few serious economists argue that war is anything other than a very costly way to achieve those goals.

how much did the second Iraq war cost?

It is notoriously difficult to accurately calculate the total cost of a war, including all the direct and indirect costs, not to mention all those lost economic opportunities. At a conservative estimate, for instance, World War I cost the global economy some $500 billion and World War II about three times as much. However, modern warfare has got exponentially more expensive.

For instance, the wars that have ravaged the Middle East for decades are estimated by the Asian thinktank Strategic Forecast Group to have cost some $12 trillion in lost GDP in the period 1991–2010. In 2013, meanwhile, the Watson Institute for International Studies at America's Brown University reported the findings of a group of 30 academics and experts on the cost of the U.S. war in Iraq since 2003. They suggested the war had cost the U.S. government $1.7 trillion, with almost a further half a billion dollars in benefits owed to war veterans. Resulting expenses, the study concluded, could exceed $6 trillion over the next four decades. Take into account the military operations in Pakistan and Afghanistan since the 9/11 attacks, and the bill rises by several trillion dollars. Nor did the report have very encouraging news on the postwar reconstruction of Iraq, with claims that most of the $212 billion earmarked for the effort had gone on security or disappeared into a black hole of waste and fraud.

economics &
the environment

For much of its history, economics has not worried unduly about its relationship with the environment. Today, however, there is a strong argument that environmental degradation poses the biggest problem that economists face.

The developed world has relied on burning fossil fuels for the last two centuries. There is a consensus among the scientific community that this has accelerated emissions of greenhouse gases to such an extent that the planet's temperature is rising with potentially devastating consequences. Melting ice caps, rising sea levels, more freak weather occurrences—all bleak prospects for the generations that follow us.

It is only since the 1980s that the issue has come to global prominence, and, for economists, it is a conundrum complete with a chicken-and-egg puzzle—how do economic activities impact the environment, and how will environmental change impact our economic activities? Any hope of beating climate change requires a unified global response, and, because many of the worst-polluting countries escape the worst of the consequences, the problem becomes thornier. Add to that the fact that pollution is generally an externality—a cost that does not accrue directly to the party causing it.

So what is to be done? Many climate skeptics—some of whom lobby on behalf of big business—suggest we should do nothing, arguing that the problem is not as big as is feared, and technology will provide a solution. Many analysts, however, remain unconvinced. William Nordhaus, a pioneering environmental economist, has predicted that climate change will inflict economic damage equivalent to 2.5% of global GDP per year by the century's end. Others offer even less optimistic prognoses. Far better, environmentalists argue, to act now to stave off future disaster.

a concerted effort?

Yet attempts to coordinate a voluntary, joint international response have reaped mixed results, as epitomized by the Kyoto Agreement formulated in 1997. Committing signatory nations to significant greenhouse-gas cuts, it was birthed in optimism but dogged by slow uptake and with targets routinely missed. Furthermore, some of the leading players would have nothing to do with it. The U.S., for instance, did not sign, arguing that its energy-hungry economy could not take it. Meanwhile, China and India refused to pick up the cost of what they considered was a problem that originated in the West. Nor have they been willing to turn their backs on fossil fuels that are powering their own stellar economic development. In addition, those countries set to suffer most at the hands of climate change—many of them in Africa and Asia and, ironically, some of the lowest pollution producers—often have the smallest voices on the international stage.

An alternative is to impose fines on polluting firms and nations, although quite how to equably and efficiently regulate such a system is yet to be established. Perhaps more hopeful is the concept of emissions trading, which echoes calls from the British economist Arthur Pigou in 1920 to tax pollution. Essentially, businesses pay for the right—perhaps by buying a government license—to emit above a certain level with a secondary market operating between firms buying and selling permits. In this way, polluters are directly incentivized to operate as cleanly as possible. It is not a perfect solution, but it is perhaps less imperfect than many of the alternatives.

what was the Stern review?

In 2006, the UK government of Tony Blair commissioned a report on the economic implications of climate change. The conclusions of its author, Nicholas Stern, a former chief economist at the World Bank, were stark. He claimed that unless emissions were reduced, there was a 75% chance that global temperatures would rise by 3.6–5.4°F within 50 years and a 50% chance that they would increase by over 9°F. Glacier melt will cause more flooding, crop yields will fall (particularly in Africa), 200 million people risk displacement from rising sea levels, and 40% of species face extinction. He predicted global GDP would likely decline by −10%, depending on the scale of temperature rise. He put the cost of addressing the problem with immediate action at 1% of GDP, and his raft of recommendations included reducing demand for heavily polluting goods and services, improving global energy supply, promoting clean energy and transport technology, and halting deforestation. Government, Stern suggested, should commit to emissions reductions, promote international carbon-trading schemes, invest in green technology, and give aid to countries worst affected by climate change.

Stern's work proved highly controversial, with his environmental and economic assessments variously accused of excessive pessimism and undue optimism. Time will tell how accurate his report is. Nonetheless, it remains a touchstone for environmental economists.

economics & religion

As with environmental considerations, economists have largely ignored the relationship between religion and economics. However, as religion continues to exert enormous social and political influence, so interest has grown in its effects upon economics.

Religion has always had things to say on economics. In the Bible, for instance, Jesus tells his disciples that it is hard for a rich man to enter the Kingdom of Heaven, whereas the parable of the talents celebrates the servant who proves himself the wiliest financial investor. Finding an economist with much to say on religion is far harder.

Adam Smith was one who did address the topic, at least to an extent. He pondered whether religious belief provided adherents with economic advantages. For example, does religion breed a climate of trust and self-regulation that reduces risk and ultimately smooths economic transactions? Put another way, would people rather do business with the godly man next door or the godless one up the street?

After Smith, relatively little was added to the debate while a consensus grew that economic development brings with it increasing secularity. It was not until the early 20th century that arguably the first great religious economist emerged. In 1905, Max Weber published *The Protestant Ethic and the Spirit of Capitalism*, in which he analyzed the relative economic development of different countries from the 16th to 19th centuries. He concluded that the Protestant nations of northern Europe and North America fared better than their Catholic counterparts in southern Europe and South America because Protestantism nurtured a work ethic and culture of frugality that was vital to the development of capitalism.

fire and brimstone

Assured that their fates were predestined, he argued, Protestants set about working hard to show their virtue and eschewed luxuries in favor of reinvesting their wealth. Catholics, meanwhile, were taught that they would earn their place in heaven by doing good works. For them, profit-motivated business was something to be regarded with suspicion, while also taking them away from good works. It is an intriguing hypothesis, although one need only look at the riches of the Spanish Empire and the Vatican to start spotting holes in the argument. For others, religious belief can convey other indirect benefits, including the promotion of strong civic institutions and improved literacy rates.

In the current century Robert Barro and Rachel McCleary analyzed economic data from some 60 countries for the period 1981–2000. They noted a trend among developing countries whereby increased belief in heaven and, especially, hell correlated to increased economic growth. It has been suggested that the prospect of eternal damnation spurred observance of the rule of law and fostered a climate of mutual trust in which business can thrive. However, it was not all good news for the established religions—if belief led to greater church attendance, economic output fell, presumably due to time being transferred from labor to religious adherence.

What is Islamic banking?

One of the most eye-catching banking success stories has been the rise of Islamic banking. At the end of 2013, the Islamic finance industry comprised over 275 institutions operating in some 75 countries. The industry was valued at $1.6 trillion in 2013, a figure predicted to increase to $4 trillion by the end of the decade. Islamic banks work in accordance with Sharia law, the moral code set out in the Koran. This means that Islamic banks cannot charge any form of interest (or *riba*), since it is prohibited to profit from borrowing or lending money. To accommodate this, Islamic banks use innovative products designed to spread risk between the financial institution and its customer. Two such commonly used instruments are *ijara* and *murabaha* schemes. An *ijara* scheme is effectively a leasing contract that is often used in place of a traditional mortgage, with the customer making regular capital and rental payments in return for an incremental transfer of ownership of a property. Under a *murabaha* scheme, rather than offering a customer a loan, the bank purchases a commodity for the customer and sells it to them at a price higher than the market value. The bank thus makes a profit to compensate for the risk of non-payment by the customer but has not charged interest. The customer repays the bank in installments, in common with a traditional loan, but in order to avoid *riba*, no extra fees, such as late charges, can be levied. Certain investments—tobacco, alcohol, and pornography—are also strictly off-limits to Islamic banks.

women count

Marilyn Waring's analysis of how Gross Domestic Product (GDP) fails to recognize the economic contribution of women around the world is considered one of the foundation texts of feminist economics.

It is difficult to overestimate the importance of GDP as a guide to an economy's health and as a tool for its policymakers. It is, after all, the figure that aims to assimilate all the economic activity that occurs within an economy during a 12-month period.

GDP has its critics (see page 110) and few economists doubt that it is an imperfect measure. However, in 1988, Marilyn Waring suggested its flaws ran very deep indeed. In her book *If Women Counted: A New Feminist Economics*, she argued that GDP is not only a gross misrepresentation of what really goes on within an economy but it is also a potent weapon used by men to reinforce outmoded patriarchal systems in society.

the invisible woman

Waring brought a systematic rigor to what was a coruscating attack on economic orthodoxy, which involved her studying how national accounts are compiled and GDP calculated in accordance with international standards. Her central thesis was that a great deal of the work undertaken around the world principally by women—from running households to looking after children, the sick, and the elderly—is invisible and goes unrecorded despite being of vital economic importance. Raising children, for instance, is economically essential, since it ensures a nation has a future labor force. Alternatively, looking after an elderly parent at home saves the state significant expense if it would otherwise be responsible for the provision of care. By the same token, the wheels of commerce would likely grind to a halt without an army of unpaid women looking after the domestic needs of the champions of industry.

Waring highlighted the illogicality of excluding work that contributes to national productivity—which is, of course, what GDP is meant to measure—simply because it is not directly remunerated. There is a certain absurdity, for instance, in including the cleaning work of a chambermaid in a guesthouse but not the similar work of a housewife, simply because the chambermaid receives a wage and the housewife does not. While it may be argued that the exclusion of unpaid labor carried out predominantly by women is simply an error of omission, Waring contended that it reflects patriarchal attempts to economically exclude, with official sanction, women in the interests of perpetuating female marginalization.

One need only look through the pages of this book to see that the academic discipline of economics has historically been the preserve of men. Marilyn Waring's work has not only provoked a significant reevaluation of how governments make their accounts and measure productivity and development but it also put wind into the sails of feminist economics.

Marilyn Waring

Marilyn Waring was born in 1952 on New Zealand's North Island. In 1973, she graduated in politics from Victoria University of Wellington. Two years later she was elected to parliament as a member of the New Zealand National Party. She was the country's youngest MP at the time and was appointed chair of the Public Expenditure Committee in 1978. Her decision to vote against the government on the question of nuclear arms and power (she supported a ban on both) effectively forced Prime Minister Robert Muldoon to call a snap election in 1984, which the National Party lost. Waring subsequently returned to academic life, and she also ran a farm for almost two decades.

If Women Counted brought her international attention in 1988 and provided the basis for the 1995 documentary film, *Who's Counting? Marilyn Waring on Sex, Lies and Global Economics,* directed by Terre Nash. In 1990, she received her doctorate in political economy from the University of Waikato and she lectured at its department of politics in the early 1990s. In 2006 she became professor of public policy at Auckland University of Technology's Institute for Public Policy, specializing in governance and public policy, political economy, gender analysis, and human rights. In 2008, she was made a Companion of the New Zealand Order of Merit for her "services to women and economics."

glossary

account A summary of economic activity over a given period.

asset A possession of value.

austerity Large-scale spending cuts undertaken by a government to address its debts.

bankruptcy A legal arrangement deployed when a subject cannot pay their debts.

bear market A market in which prices are likely to fall. *See also* bull market.

billion A thousand million.

bond An investor loan to a government or business for a defined time period at a fixed rate of interest.

boom A period of strong economic activity.

BRICS nations Acronym referring to the emerging economies of Brazil, Russia, India, China, and, latterly, South Africa.

bubble A cumulative rise in price driven principally by a belief that the price will rise further.

budget A government statement of expenditures and receipts for the coming year(s).

bull market A market in which prices are likely to rise. *See also* bear market.

business All forms of commercial activity (also referring to any organization involved therein).

bust A sudden economic collapse.

capital Manmade resources used in economic production.

capitalism Economic system based on the private ownership of property and the means of production.

central bank The bank that controls a country's money supply and its monetary policy.

command economy Economy controlled by a centralized decision-making body.

commodity Raw material that can be traded in bulk.

competition The state of individual buyers and sellers having a choice of suppliers and customers.

consumption The use of goods and services to satisfy needs and wants.

cost The sacrifice resulting from making a particular decision.

crash A sudden decline in the value of a market.

credit The supply of a good or service for a deferred payment.

credit union A cooperative financial institution.

currency The money in general use in a country or regional block.

debt Money owed by one party to another.

deficit An excess of liabilities over assets over a set period of time.

deflation A progressive fall in price level.

demand The wish and ability to acquire a good or service.

Depression An extended period of low economic activity and high unemployment.

derivative A tradable security, the value of which is decided by the price of an underlying asset.

developed economy A country with established high levels of economic growth, security, and general living standards.

developing economy A country with generally lower levels of income, living standards, and social indicators.

dividend Payment made by a business to its shareholders, usually on an annual basis.

economic cycle General pattern of fluctuations in a national economy, such as expansion, peak, recession, and recovery.

economics Social science looking at how individuals and groups use scarce resources to meet their needs and wants.

economy System of production, distribution, and consumption of goods and services.

employment Service or trade performed for payment under contract of hire.

equilibrium The state in which the forces of demand and supply are in perfect balance.

equities Stocks and shares in a private company.

Eurozone Comprising those European Union (EU) member nations who have adopted the euro as their currency.

exchange rate The value of one currency against another.

expenditure Spending, either by a consumer, government, or investor.

exports Goods and services sold by one economy to another.

Federal Reserve The system of central banking in the USA.

finance The creation, management, and study of money (or, alternatively, monetary support for an enterprise).

financial sector The part of the economy made up of banks and other financial institutions.

fiscal policy Government policy on taxation and expenditure.

foreign exchange The money of a foreign country.

free market An economy based on market instruments and free from state intervention.

GDP Gross Domestic Product, a measure of economic activity valuing all the final goods and services produced in an economy over a given time. *See also* GNP.

GINI coefficient Statistical measure of inequality.

globalization The process of worldwide integration of social, cultural, and economic systems.

GNP Gross National Product, a measure of economic activity equivalent to GDP (see above) plus net income from abroad.

gold standard A system that fixes international exchange rates by making currencies convertible into gold at a fixed price.

growth Increased capacity to produce goods and services within an economy over a given period.

heterodox economics Economic thought outside of the mainstream.

hyperinflation Rapid inflation that threatens the position of a currency as a means of exchange.

ILO International Labour Organization, a United Nations agency concerned with labour matters and human rights.

IMF International Monetary Fund, a United Nations agency promoting international monetary cooperation and stability.

imports Goods and services bought by one economy from another.

income Money or other assets received.

inequality Differences in the distribution of money within a given economic system.

inflation A persistent trend of rising prices.

informal economy Unregulated economic activity.

insurance A contractual agreement to spread and reduce risk.

interest Payment owed to a lender in excess of the amount borrowed.

International Bank for Reconstruction and Development *See* World Bank.

investment A monetary asset purchased to provide a future income or to be sold for profit.

liability A legal obligation to make a payment.

loan A sum lent and to be returned, usually with interest.

loss The outcome when expenditure exceeds income.

macroeconomics The study of large-scale economic factors.

market A forum for buying and selling.

market economy An economy in which a significant proportion of goods and services are allocated via the market.

microeconomics The study of the behavior of individual consumers and businesses.

microfinance Banking services provided to those on low incomes who have limited or no access to traditional financial service providers.

mixed economy An economy combining aspects of public and private enterprise.

monetary policy Government or central bank policy that manipulates interest rates or money supply to influence the economy.

money A medium of exchange and store of value.

monopoly Where a single organization controls an entire market for a good or service.

multinational Operating across more than one country.

national debt The full extent of debt owed by a national government.

nationalization The process of bringing a private enterprise under government ownership.

not-for-profit Description of an organization where all monies received are reallocated for the pursuance of its objectives and not as profit for its owners.

OECD Organization for Economic Cooperation and Development, a group of 30 free-market economies.

oligopoly Where a small group of businesses controls an entire market for a good or service.

opportunity cost The next-best opportunity given up by making a particular choice.

orthodox economics Mainstream economic thought.

per capita For each person.

planned economy An economy in which the majority of goods and services are allocated via a centralized authority.

poverty The state of being unable to afford life's essentials.

price The amount of money paid for a good or service.

primary sector The part of an economy that makes use of natural resources.

private sector Those parts of the economy not under government control.

privatization The transfer to private ownership of assets and enterprises formerly under government control.

profit The excess of receipts over expenditure for a business over a set period.

protectionism Government policies designed to protect domestic industry from international competition.

public sector Those parts of the economy not controlled by private individuals or organizations.

recession A general decline in economic activity, usually observed by successive falls in GDP (see that entry above).

recovery The movement of an economy from its lowest point back toward normal levels.

regulation Rules that individuals or organizations are obliged to observe.

resources Any assets that can contribute to economic activity.

return The proceeds or profit received from an economic undertaking.

risk Uncertainty over the size of return on an investment.

saving Income not spent on consumption in a given period.

scarcity A shortage of something that is in demand.

secondary sector That part of an economy encompassing manufacturing, processing, and construction.

security Something pledged to guarantee the fulfillment of an economic undertaking, or a financial instrument representing ownership of a stock, share, bond, etc.

share A part ownership of an enterprise.

single currency A currency used by more than one country—for example, the euro.

state-owned An entity whose ownership lies with the state, usually represented by the government.

stock A synonym for share, or alternatively a store of goods built up by an enterprise.

stock exchange (or stock market) An institution where stocks and shares are sold.

supply The amount of a good or service on sale.

supranational Transcending national borders.

surplus An excess of assets over liabilities over a set period of time.

taxation Compulsory payments to the government made by individuals and organizations.

tertiary sector That part of an economy encompassing service industries.

trade The basic act of buying and selling.

Treasury The funds or revenues of a state, or the government department overseeing them.

trillion A million million (or a thousand billion).

UN United Nations, an organization that aims for international cooperation and peace and which has a membership comprising every recognized nation state—with the exception of the Vatican City.

utility Satisfaction gained by consuming a good or service.

wages Payment for work performed for an employer.

wealth Total value of assets of an individual, organization, or country minus all debts.

World Bank A supranational body established in 1946 to promote economic cooperation and development.

WTO World Trade Organization, an organization that governs the rules of international trade.

bibliography

Arrow, Kenneth J., *Social Choice and Individual Values* (Yale University Press, 1951)

Becker, Gary, *Human Capital: A Theoretical and Empirical Analysis with Special Reference to Education* (University of Chicago Press, 1994; originally published 1964)

Bergmann, Barbara, *The Economic Emergence of Women* (Basic Books, 1986)

Black, John, Hashimzade, Nigar, and Myles, Gareth, *A Dictionary of Economics* (Oxford University Press, 2012)

Blyth, Mark, *Austerity: The History of a Dangerous Idea* (Oxford University Press, 2013)

Dubner, Stephen J. & Levitt, Steven D., *Freakonomics: A Rogue Economist Explores the Hidden Side of Everything* (William Morrow, 2005)

Durlauf, Steven N. and Blum, Lawrence E. (eds), *The New Palgrave Dictionary of Economics* (Palgrave Macmillan, 2008)

Erickson, Jon D. & Farley, Joshua, *Ecological Economics: Principles and Applications* (Island Press, 2003)

Friedman, Milton, *Capitalism and Freedom* (University of Chicago Press, 2002; originally published 1962)

Galbraith, John Kenneth, *The Affluent Society* (Penguin, 1999; originally published 1958)

George, Henry, *Progress and Poverty* (Schalkenbach (Robert) Foundation, 2006; originally published 1879)

Hayek, Friedrich, *The Road to Serfdom* (Routledge, 2001; originally published 1944)

Heilbroner, Robert, *The Worldly Philosophers: The Lives, Times and Ideas of the Great Economic Thinkers* (Touchstone, 1999; originally published 1953)

Kahneman, Daniel, *Thinking, Fast and Slow* (Penguin, 2012)

Keynes, John Maynard, *General Theory of Employment, Interest and Money* (Mariner Books, 1965; originally published 1936)

Kindleberger, Charles P., *Manias, Panics, and Crashes: A History of Financial Crises* (Macmillan, 1978)

Krugman, Paul, *The Return of Depression Economics* (Allen Lane, 2008)

Kuznets, Simon, *Modern Economic Growth: Rate, Structure and Spread* (Yale University Press, 1966)

Malthus, Thomas, *An Essay on the Principle of Population* (Penguin Books Ltd, 1982; originally published 1798)

Marshall, Alfred, *Principles of Economics* (Palgrave Macmillan, 2013; originally published 1890)

Marx, Karl, *Capital: A Critique of Political Economy Vols I-III* (Penguin Classics, 1990–92; originally published 1867–94)

Menger, Carl, *Principles of Economics* (Terra Libertas Limited, 2011; originally published 1871)

Mill, John Stuart, *Principles of Political Economy* (Penguin Classics, 1985; originally published 1848)

von Mises, Ludwig, *Human Action* (Ludwig von Mises Institute, 2010; originally published 1949)

Morgenstern, Oskar and von Neumann, John, *Theory of Games and Economic Behavior* (Princeton University Press, 2007; originally published 1944)

Nash, John (ed. Harold Kuhn and Sylvia Nasar), *The Essential John Nash* (Princeton University Press, 2007)

North, Douglass C. and Thomas, Robert Paul, *The Rise of the Western World: A New Economic History* (Cambridge University Press, 1973)

Pareto, Vilfredo, *Manual of Political Economy* (Oxford University Press, 2014; originally published 1906)

Pickett, Kate and Wilkinson, Richard, *The Spirit Level: Why More Equal Societies Almost Always Do Better* (Allen Lane, 2009)

Pigou, Arthur Cecil, *The Economics of Welfare* (Transaction Publishers, 2001; originally published 1920)

Piketty, Thomas, *Capital in the Twenty-First Century* (Harvard University Press, 2014)

Polanyi, K., *The Great Transformation* (Farrar & Rinehart, 1944)

Potter, Beatrice, *The Co-operative Movement in Great Britain* (Scholar's Choice, 2015; originally published 1891)

Prebisch, Raul, *The Economic Development of Latin America and Its Principal Problems* (Economic Commission for Latin America, 1950)

Ricardo, David, *Principles of Political Economy and Taxation* (Dover Publications Inc., 2004; originally published 1817)

Sachs, Jeffrey, *The End of Poverty: Economic Possibilities for Our Time* (Penguin Press, 2005)

Samuelson, Paul A., *Foundations of Economic Analysis* (Harvard University Press, 1947)

Schumpeter, Joseph, *Capitalism, Socialism and Democracy* (Routledge, 2010; originally published 1942)

Sen, Amartya, *Poverty and Famines: An Essay on Entitlement and Deprivation* (Oxford University Press, 1981)

Shiller, Robert J., *Irrational Exuberance* (Princeton University Press, 2000)

Smith, Adam, *An Inquiry into the Nature and Causes of the Wealth of Nations* (Wordsworth Editions, 2012; originally published 1776)

Sowell, Thomas, *Is Reality Optional? and Other Essays* (Hoover Institution Press, 1993)

Stiglitz, Joseph, *Globalization and Its Discontents* (W. W. Norton & Co., 2002)

Veblen, Thorstein, *The Theory of the Leisure Class* (Oxford University Press, 2009; originally published 1899)

Walras, Léon, *Elements of Theoretical Economics: Or, The Theory of Social Wealth* (Cambridge University Press, 2014; originally published 1874)

Waring, Marilyn, *If Women Counted: A New Feminist Economics* (Harper & Row, 1988)

index

accounting profits 65
Africa, sub-Saharan 159
agricultural economies 38, 39
Akerloff, George 82
Alesina, Alberto 41
Andersen, Arthur 55
antidumping laws 148
antimonopolistic (antitrust)
    legislation 78
Austrian School 29, 114, 115

balance of trade 144–5
balance sheets 54
Ban Ki-moon 157
Bank for International
    Settlements 121
Bank of England 120
bankruptcy 102–3
banks
    central 88, 120–1
    commercial 88
    investment 88–9
    Islamic 183
    Lehman Brothers 103, 167
    LIBOR scandal 33
    merchant 88–9
    microfinance 97
    nationalization 130
    private 89
    retail 88
    supranational 88, 162–3
    types of 88–9
    see also individual banks
Baran, Paul 153
Barro, Robert 183
barter systems 13
bear markets 49
Beautiful Mind, A (film) 75
Becker, Gary 106–7
behavioral economics 73
Bentham, Jeremy 63, 147
bequests 100–1
Berle, Adolf 80
Bernanke, Ben 91, 119
bitcoins 141
black market 154–5
Bloomberg Platform 83
bond markets 33

Boody, Elizabeth 47
boom-and-bust cycles 44–5
Booth, Charles 134
bottom line 65
Bretton Woods Agreement
    95, 145, 162
BRICS 111
Brown, Gordon 45
bubbles 48–9
Buffett, Warren 105
bull markets 49
business cycles 45

capital 36–7
capital gains tax 126
Carlyle, Thomas 15
cashflow statements 55
Celebrity Net Worth 51
charitable giving 104–5
Chávez, Hugo 113
China 39, 91, 111, 149, 157,
    173, 181
Churchill, Winston 100
classical economics 16
climate change 180–1
collective bargaining 134–5
command economies 112–13
commodities market 33
common ownership 36
companies
    executive pay 81
    small/large 70–2
    types of 76–9
comparative advantage
    146–7
compound interest 91
consumers
consumer surplus 34
Corn Laws (1815) 146
corporate governance 80–1
corporate tax 126
creative destruction 46–7
credit 92–3
credit crunch 166
credit-ratings agencies 139
credit unions 92
crowdfunding 97
currencies
    origins 13
    values 140–1
currency crises 141

dark web 155
Darwin, Charles 175
death duties see estate tax;
    inheritance tax
deflation 122
delayed gratification 19
demographics 172–3
dependency theory 152–3
developed nations 156–7
developing nations 156–9
    see also dependency theory
Di Modica, Arturo 49
Dickens, Charles 101
diminishing returns 68–9
disinflation 122
division of labor 133
dot.com bubble 48
double-entry bookkeeping 55
Dresher, Melvin 74
Dunoyer, Charles 45

e-commerce 77
Easterlin, Richard 110
eBay 77
economic bubbles 48–9
economic forecasting 56–7
Economic Man 72–3, 95
economic model, the 56
economic profits 65
economies of scale 70–2
Einstein, Albert 126
Engels, Friedrich 67
Enron 55
entitlement theory 160–1
environmental economics 29,
    180–1
environmental Kuznets
    curve 41
equilibrium 61
equities market 33
equity 54
Essmart 105
estate tax 100
Eurozone crisis 167
exchange-rate manipulation
    148
executive pay 81
export subsidies 148

FDI (Foreign Direct
Investment) 144

feminist economics 29
    see also Waring, Marilyn
financial accounting 54–5
financial markets 32–3
Fitoussi, Jean-Paul 110
fixed costs 68
Flash Crash (2010) 83
Flood, Merrill 74
Ford, Henry 71, 102
forecasting 56–7
foreign aid 159
Foreign Direct Investment
    (FDI) 144
foreign exchange 141
foreign exchange market 33
Frank, Andre Gunder 153
Franklin, Benjamin 26, 51, 101
free-market economies
    15–17, 63
Friedman, Milton 91, 115,
    123, 124–5, 137
Frisch, Ragnar 56
Fukuyama, Francis 57
Furtado, Celso 153

G20 149
game theory 74–5
Gates, Bill 51, 52, 79, 105
    Bill and Melinda Gates
    Foundation 52, 104
GATT (General Agreement
    on Tariffs and Trade) 145
GDP (Gross Domestic
    Product) 110, 184–5
genetically modified (GM)
    crops 20
"gilt-edged" bonds 33
Giving Pledge 105
Gleick, Peter 21
globalization 150–1
GNP (Gross National
    Product) 110
gold standard 95, 120–1,
    140
Goldman Sachs 78
Grameen Bank 97
great moderation, the 119
Great Recession (2008–13)
    23, 48, 57, 130, 166–9
Gross Domestic Product
    (GDP) 110, 184–5

Gross National Product (GNP) 110
gross pension replacement rate 98
growth 42–5, 43

Hanseatic League 151
Hayek, Friedrich 29, 114–15
healthcare 128, 129
hedge funds 88
heterodox economics 28–9
hidden economy 154–5
High Frequency Trades 83
HNWIs (high-net-worth individuals) 89
housing market
  as economic indicator 44
  as investment 95
human capital 37
Hume, David 15, 175
hyperinflation 122

IBRD (International Bank for Reconstruction) 162
Icelandic banks 130
IMF (International Monetary Fund) 162–3
import quotas 148
import substitution industrialization (ISI) 153
income 50
income tax 126, 127
industrial economies 38–9
Industrial Revolution 14, 36, 38–9, 46, 134
inflation 122–3
informal economy 154–5
information, access to 82–3
inheritance tax 100
insider dealing 83
insolvency 102–3
installment plans 92
International Bank for Reconstruction (IBRD) 162
International Monetary Fund (IMF) 162–3
international trade 144–5
  see also globalization
internet
  dot.com bubble 48
  and illegal trade 155

and the new economy 39
and search frictions 77
"investment grade" bonds 33
investments 94–5
"invisible hand" 17
ISI (import substitution industrialization) 153
Islamic banking 183

Jigme Singye Wangchuck, 111
Jobs, Steve 81
"junk" bonds 33

Kahneman, Daniel 72, 73
Keynes, John Maynard 130, 137, 169, 170–1, 175
Kickstarter (website) 97
Koch, Fred 101
Kuznets curve 40–1
Kuznets, Simon 41
Kydland, Finn 121
Kyoto Agreement 180–1

labor force 132–3
labor theory of value 25, 66–7
laissez-faire 16, 62
Lausanne School 85
Lay, Kenneth 55
leading indicators 56
least developed countries (LDC) 157
Lehman Brothers 103, 167
LIBOR scandal 33

McCleary, Rachel 183
macroeconomics 22–3
mainstream economics see orthodox economics
Malthus, Thomas 16, 147, 174–5
management accounting 54
Mansa Musa I 51
marginal utility 19
marginalism 34
market value 24–5
markets, types of 32–3
Marshall, Alfred 34–5
Marshall, Howard, II 101
Marx, Karl 16, 25, 29, 36, 37, 46, 47, 66–7, 112, 133,

136–7, 175
MDGs (Millennium Development Goals) 157
Means, Gardiner 80
Menger, Carl 29
mercantilism 14, 144, 146
microeconomics 22–3
microfinance 96–7
Microsoft 78, 79
Mill, James 63, 147
Mill, John Stuart 16, 62–3
Millennium Development Goals (MDGs) 157
Mincer, Jacob 106
minimum wage 132
Mises, Ludwig von 115
Modigliani, Franco 91
monetarism 124–5
money, invention of 13
money markets 32–3
money supply 118–19
monopolies 78–9
Morgenstern, Oskar 74
multinationals 150–1

Nash, John 74, 75
national debt 138–9
nationalization 130–1
natural monopolies 79
neoclassical economics 34–5
neoclassical synthesis 28
neoliberals 115
Neumann, John von 74
Neuwirth, Robert 155
new economy, the 39
New Home Economics 107
Nixon, Richard 145
Nobel Prize for Economics 29
Nordhaus, William 180

Obama, President Barack 129
occupational pensions 98
oligopolies 78
opportunity cost 26–7
options 32
orthodox economics 28–9
Ostrum, Elinor 29
overdrafts 92

Pacioli, Luca 55
Paley, Mary 35

Pareto, Vilfredo 84–5
patents 148
payday loans 92
payroll tax 126
Pebble E-Paper Watch 97
pensions 98–9, 176–7
perfect competition 34–5
philanthropy 52, 104–5
Philipps, Bill 123
Pigou, Arthur 181
PPF (Production Possibility Frontier) 84, 116–17
PPP (Purchasing Power Parity) dollars 50
Prebisch, Raúl 152–3
Prescott, Edward 121
prisoner's dilemma, the 74–5
private companies 78
private pensions 98
private property 36–7
privatization 131
Production Possibility Frontier (PPF) 84, 116–17
profit-and-loss accounts 54
profits 64–5
property market
  as economic indicator 44
  investment in 95
  property tax 126
protectionism 148–9
public companies 77, 78
public goods/services 128–31
Purchasing Power Parity (PPP) dollars 50

quantitative easing (QE) 167–9

rational/irrational consumer 72
religion 182–3
representative firms 34
revolving credit 92–3
Ricardo, David 16, 25, 146–7, 175
Riksbank, Sveriges 29
risk and consumers 72, 95
Robbins, Lionel 26
Rockefeller, John D. 51, 78–9
Rodrik, Dani 41
Rosenstein-Rodan, Paul 158

Rothschild, Mayer Amschel 119
Rothschild, Nathan 83
rotten kid theorem 107
Rousseau, Jean-Jacques 175

Sachs, Jeffrey 139
Saez, Emmanuel 53
sales tax 126
Santayana, George 57
savings 90–1
scarcity 20–1
Schliff, Peter 57
Schumpeter, Joseph 46–7
search frictions 77
Sen, Amartya 110, 160–1
service economies 39
shadow economy 154–5
Silk Road
  (dark website) 155
Simon, Herbert 73
Singer, Hans 152–3
SIRUM 105
Sismondi, Jean-Charles 45

Smith, Adam 14–17, 44, 72, 133, 146, 182
Smith, Anna Nicole 101
social enterprises 105
social-market economies 113
sole traders 76
stagflation 123
Stalin, Joseph 113
state-owned companies 76
state pensions 98
Stern Review 181
Stiglitz, Joseph 110, 163, 178
Stock, James 119
subprime mortgages 48, 57, 103
subsidies 148
supply and demand 60–1
sustainable growth 42–5
Swope, Gerard 93

tariffs 148
tax avoidance 127
tax evasion 127
taxes 126–7

Taylor, Harriet 63
time-series data 56
trade unions 134–5
trade wars 149
trading blocs 151
trusts 100
Tversky, Amos 72, 73

Ulbricht, Ross 155
underground economy 154–5
unemployment 136–7
utility 18–19

value 24–5
variable costs 68
Voltaire 15

Walmart 150
war 178–9
Waring, Marilyn 184–5
Washington Consensus 158
water resources 21
Watson, Mark 119

wealth
  definition 50–1
  distribution 53
Webb, Beatrice 134–5
Webb, Sidney 134
Weber, Max 182
Wieser, Friedrich von 26
wills 100–1
women
  feminist economics 29
  unpaid labor of 184–5
  in the workforce 173
  working hours 133
World Bank 97, 162
World Trade Organization (WTO) 145
WorldCom 55

Yunus, Muhammad 97

zero growth 43
Zucman, Gabriel 53

acknowledgments

© Alamy | Daily Mail/Rex 153 | epa european pressphoto agency b.v. 107 | INTERFOTO 35, 85
© Creative Commons 47, 52, 71, 155, 125, 135, 147, 161, 175
© Getty | Walter Sanders 171
© iStock | thumb 57, 71, 130, 167
© Shutterstock |12_Tribes 57 | 61059715 163 | aarrows 173 | aastock 163 | Africa Studio 16 | albert_kremenko 13| Alex Staroseltsev 25 | allanw 99 | Andrey_Popov 58 | Antonov Roman 83 | Aris Suwanmalee 101 | Artgraphixel 111 | Arthimedes 174 | autsawin uttisin 141 | BortN66 74 | Chamille White 133 | Christin Lola 184 | corund 108 | Creative Stall 33, 95, 149, 169 | Croisy 24 | Cube29 111, 145 | cybrain 157 | Dan Kosmayer 149 | Darren Pullman 177 | Darq 83 | dekede 164 | Dmitry Zimin 90 | Dudarev Mikhail 43 | EpicStockMedia 177 | Eric Isselee 13| Evan Lorne 13 | Everett Historical 15, 63, 67 | Evgeny Atamanenko 93 | Everything 84 | Gajus 101 | geraria 65 | Giuliano Del Moretto 177 | Globe Turner 111 | Godunova Tatiana 19 | Gts 118 | Gumenyuk Dmitriy 133 | Gunnar Pippel 127 | Gwoeii 71 | Haver 49 | hecho 37 | hidesy 121, 178 | hin255 169 | holbox 13 | iadams 22 | icons_man 52, 102, 105 | IERSHOVA KHRYSTYNA 95 | ImageFlow 123 | Isa Ismail 21 | isak55 83 | iunewind 21 | James.Pintar 16 | jannoon028 77 | Jne Valokuvaus 99 | JOAT 183 | JPC-PROD 52 | JRMurray76 22 | Julia Tsokur 155 | Julinzy 111 | Kazlouski Siarhei p.38 | Konstantin Gushcha 69 | Konstantinos Kokkinis 52 | Kostsov 142, 181 | koya979 150 | Krivosheev Vitaly 83 | kurhan 99 | Khvost 117 | life_in_a_pixel 81 | Lisa S. 37 | LovePHY 38 | Lynn Y 21 | margouillat photo 77 | Mariyana M 24 | Mark Herreid 112 | Maxx-Studio 73 | Maryna Pleshkun 163 | mikeledray 96 | Mikko Lemola 155 | minifilm 123 | Mmaxer 89 | Natali Zakharova 77 | Natykach Nataliia 65 | NEGOVURA 170 | Nikodash 133 | nito 137 | oixpert 164 | Ollyy 173 | Pavel Ignatov 155 | Picsfive 139 | Production Perig 129 | Rawpixel.com 32 | researcher97 23 | Richard Peterson 117 | Rob Wilson 37 | Rybakov Vadim Grigor'evich 129 | Sandra Cunningham 65 | Sasha_Gromov 49 | sfam_photo 129 | Singkham 156 | Skylines 86 | Slavko Sereda 113 | Smit 51 | Spotmatik Ltd 38 | Stuart Monk 49 | studioVin 26 | Subbotina Anna 43 | Suzanne Tucker 43 | Syda Productions 55 | Take Photo 160 | Tatiana Popova 141 | TheaDesign 105 | Thomas Pajot 111 | TijanaM 55 | tovovan 21 | urfin 10 | Vadim Georgiev 101 | valdis torms 30 | VGstockstudio 123 | violetkaipa 79 | Vitalii Tiagunov 26 | Vitezslav Valka 28| wacomka 24 | yanugkelid 75

Illustrations by Simon Daley.

All other images are in the public domain.

Every effort has been made to credit the copyright holders of the images used in this book. We apologize for any unintentional omissions or errors and will insert the appropriate acknowledgment to any companies or individuals in subsequent editions of the work.